She Means Business

She Means Business

Turn Your Ideas into Reality and Become a Wildly Successful Entrepreneur

CARRIE GREEN

HAY HOUSE

Carlsbad, California • New York City • London
Sydney •Johannesburg • Vancouver • New Delhi

First published and distributed in the United Kingdom by:
Hay House UK Ltd, Astley House, 33 Notting Hill Gate, London W11 3JQ
Tel: +44 (0)20 3675 2450; Fax: +44 (0)20 3675 2451; www.hayhouse.co.uk

Published and distributed in the United States of America by:
Hay House Inc., PO Box 5100, Carlsbad, CA 92018-5100
Tel: (1) 760 431 7695 or (800) 654 5126; Fax: (1) 760 431 6948 or (800) 650 5115
www.hayhouse.com

Published and distributed in Australia by:
Hay House Australia Ltd, 18/36 Ralph St, Alexandria NSW 2015
Tel: (61) 2 9669 4299; Fax: (61) 2 9669 4144; www.hayhouse.com.au

Published and distributed in the Republic of South Africa by:
Hay House SA (Pty) Ltd, PO Box 990, Witkoppen 2068
info@hayhouse.co.za; www.hayhouse.co.za

Published and distributed in India by:
Hay House Publishers India, Muskaan Complex, Plot No.3, B-2,
Vasant Kunj, New Delhi 110 070
Tel: (91) 11 4176 1620; Fax: (91) 11 4176 1630; www.hayhouse.co.in

Distributed in Canada by:
Raincoast Books, 2440 Viking Way, Richmond, B.C. V6V 1N2
Tel: (1) 604 448 7100; Fax: (1) 604 270 7161; www.raincoast.com

Text © Carrie Green, 2017

The moral rights of the author have been asserted.

The information given in this book should not be treated as a substitute for professional
medical advice; always consult a medical practitioner. Any use of information in this book
is at the reader's discretion and risk. Neither the author nor the publisher can be held
responsible for any loss, claim or damage arising out of the use, or misuse, of the suggestions
made, the failure to take medical advice or for any material on third party websites.

A catalogue record for this book is available from the British Library.

ISBN: 978-1-78180-740-8

Printed and bound in Great Britain by
TJ International Ltd, Padstow, Cornwall

MIX
Paper from
responsible sources
FSC
www.fsc.org   FSC® C013056

*To everyone that has supported me throughout
my entrepreneurial journey, this is for you.*

*Mum and Dad, thank you for opening my mind and
making me believe that anything is possible. My siblings,
Sam, James, and Nick, thank you for cheering me on and
making the adventure fun. My husband, Kelin, thank you
for your pep talks, they're the best! To all of my friends, FEA
members and followers – thank you for believing in me.*

I love you all.

CONTENTS

Contents

Who is she?

She is brave, courageous, a real go-getter.

She knows what she wants and she knows that
she'll make it happen.

She stays positive even when times are hard.

She surrounds herself with like-minded people who
want her to succeed.

She learns all she can to help her strive forward.

Nothing is going to stop her from making her
dreams come true.

SHE MEANS BUSINESS.

THIS IS NO ACCIDENT

Hello lovely, I'm so delighted that my book has made its way into your hands. It's pretty crazy to think that in this huge world, with its seven-billion-plus people, our paths have crossed.

Maybe the book jumped out at you from the bookstore shelf, or maybe a friend gave it to you, or perhaps you already know of me through the Female Entrepreneur Association (FEA) and wanted to find out more.

However it happened, I don't believe that you're reading this book by accident – the universe just doesn't work that way.

I reckon you're here because you've got something wonderful to offer the world and maybe want some inspiration to help you rise up, get your message out there, and build a successful business. Maybe it's because you want to live a life doing something you love, doing something that means something to you and to others, or creating something that will give you the freedom to work from where you want, when you want.

Am I right? If so, you have everything you need in your hands and we're going to dream big together, get inspired, and bond over the crazy entrepreneurial journey!

In the following pages, I'm going to challenge you to up-level your business and life, get your ideas and messages out into the world, and make amazing things happen. I'll share with you all the advice that I wish I'd had when I started out on this journey, lots of ideas to help you take action, and a few stories of other women who are doing some amazing things on their entrepreneurial journey.

You'll hear about my incredible sister, Samantha Costello – founder of The Little Green Studio, a luxury wedding stationery range; my best friend from university, Ailish Lucas – creator of the organic beauty blog, The Glow Getter; my amazing FEA teammate, Michelle Rohr – founder of The Secret O.W.L. Society, who sells her printables on Etsy; my good friend all the way from Hawaii, Nikki Elledge Brown – founder of A Course About Copy; and the amazing Kimra Luna – the creator of Be True, Brand You and the founder of Freedom Hackers.

All of these women come from a different background and run different businesses, but their stories show what's possible. This book is not just one person leveraging the Internet to get her message and business out there, this is a movement with millions of women involved, and the opportunities are yours for the taking too.

At the end of the book you'll find my 28-Day She Means Business Challenge to help you get your ideas out into the world. There's also a workbook and free online course that accompanies this book to help you take action; you can access it at http://bit.ly/SMB-Resources

While I don't know what stage of business you're at, I am 100 percent sure that you can build a successful one.

How can I be so certain?

If other people can build a successful business, despite the fact that they once felt confused and overwhelmed by the seemingly mammoth tasks that lay ahead, you can too, right?

Right.

And I'm going to show you how you can do it.

HOW TO USE THIS BOOK

Use this book however you feel guided to use it. Read through it in one go, open the book at a random page and see what message comes your way, write in it, mark the pages, take pictures of your favorite sections... do whatever you like.

This is yours, so squeeze as much out of it as you can :-)

THANK YOU INTERNET

I'd like to pause before we set off and thank the Internet for being so magnificent in allowing so many more people to take their genius ideas and messages and turn them into successful businesses.

Thanks to the Internet, you can live anywhere you want and if you have a computer and an Internet connection you can build a successful business, and impact millions of people from around the world. That is pretty incredible.

I see people doing this every single day, and it's something I've experienced firsthand too.

I started my first business in 2005 at the age of 19, when I'd run out of money after my first year of university! A very random opportunity came up for me to start an online phone unlocking business (which was legal, I checked!)

I had absolutely zero knowledge of how to build a business (and no money!), but within four years I'd learned how to make it a success. We had 100,000+ visits to the website every month, 500,000+ views on our YouTube channel, and were generating revenue of $50,000 a month.

I'd woken up to a powerful realization:

The Internet is a goldmine that EVERYONE can tap into, even if they don't know how just yet.

That being said, my entrepreneurial journey has had its fair share of ups and downs. In fact, while building my first business, I ended up feeling completely isolated and lonely. After going around in circles for a long time (more on that later) I decided to build a platform, the Female Entrepreneur Association (FEA), to bring together female entrepreneurs from around the world, so we could inspire and empower each other to succeed.

I started FEA with zero fans, followers, and traffic, as well as with no clue how to build an online community to support women in business or a network. What I did have was a big vision and lots of determination to figure it out and make it happen.

Within five years we had 300,000+ fans on Facebook, 100,000+ email subscribers, 80,000+ visits to our website each month, and the business was generating more than $90,000 per month.

Replicating the success of the first business wasn't an accident. I did it on purpose, by taking specific actions, which I'll be sharing with you in this book.

Has it been easy? Hmmmm, let's just say it's been a rollercoaster of an adventure!

Can we all create success like this and beyond? Absolutely, I'm going to show you how.

Will it be worth it? YES.

Through FEA, I've come to know many women with similar stories, and I'll be telling you about their journeys too, but first let me tell you about my amazing friend Michelle Rohr.

Michelle lives on the tiny island of Guam, in the middle of the Pacific Ocean. She had a niggle – a feeling deep down that she wanted to do more with her life, even though at the beginning she didn't know what that meant. Over a few years she worked on following her inner knowing, which then transformed into ideas and her ideas transformed into her business. As I write these words, she's created so much success that she's been able to quit her other jobs and just focus on building her businesses, from home. Michelle is creating her dream life.

Every time she makes a sale through her Etsy store her iPhone makes a cha-ching noise… while she works, while she relaxes, while she sleeps. *Cha-ching, cha-ching, cha-ching.*

Her little sister once asked her, 'How do you make money? You're always home.'

Oh, how I love the Internet.

Michelle has turned her niggle into a successful business, by using the Internet to gather together a group of like-minded people, who love what she does and what she offers. So, not only has she built a successful business, she's also doing something which is having such a positive impact on people, which makes her feel more fulfilled and adds more meaning to her life.

This is the power of the Internet, and the possibilities are endless.

Seriously.

I'm not talking about just creating small businesses here, but mind-blowingly successful, amazing businesses (if you want to).

You may or may not have heard of Marie Forleo, but in the online business world, she's a big deal. She is someone whose idea met the Internet, and she leveraged it to explode her business to eight figures. On top of that, she's making a positive impact on people all over the world and doing what she loves.

Or take Kimra Luna, who within a year of starting her online business was closing in on making her first million, while raising two children and pregnant with her third. Again, she was doing something that she loved too.

So much is possible… for every single one of us. It's ridiculously exciting.

But let's be real.

Even though the Internet has provided us with an incredibly exciting proposition to turn our ideas into realities, it's not exactly a walk in the park. (Yes, thank you Facebook Ads, webinars, social media, and so many other things for making us entrepreneurs feel like we're crazy, overwhelmed people!) Sometimes, it's hard to even know where to begin when you're trying to turn an idea that was in your head into reality.

There are a million and one things to do, most of which you haven't got a clue how to do, and it feels incredibly overwhelming, confusing, and sometimes even hopeless. Yet, despite it all, we choose to persevere, even without the guarantee that it will actually work.

This, my friend, is what makes us feel like we're completely crazy.

It's a daring adventure, so buckle up and get ready for it…

SHE SETS OFF ON HER ENTREPRENEURIAL JOURNEY

We like to think the journey will look like this…

But it actually looks more like this…

The entrepreneurial journey is a big adventure.

We're daring trailblazers, on a journey that takes us so far outside of our comfort zone that at some point or another the thought, 'Am I crazy?!' will inevitably cross our mind. In the 10-plus years of being on my entrepreneurial journey, it's definitely been a recurring thought of mine.

In fact, it was exactly how I was feeling in February of 2011. The winter that had just passed seemed more gloomy than normal; everything seemed grayer and more miserable! There was one reason for this: I wasn't happy. In fact I was totally miserable.

I had reached the end of my tether with everything and I felt hopeless. I often wonder how I'd let it get that far, but I guess these things happen.

Just under six years earlier…

I was going into my second year of studying Law at university. During my first year I'd spent more money that I actually had… like most students! Not only had I reached my overdraft limit, I had spent the whole of my student loan for that year too (on clothes I might add!). So when an opportunity came about to start a business I was more than interested.

The business was mobile phone unlocking – at the time I didn't even know what mobile unlocking was! I had no real clue about business either, but I had nothing to lose so I got started.

I came up with a name, bought the domain, and put a terrible website together myself. Then I discovered that I could set up a Google AdWords account and create ads to drive traffic to my website. You may be wondering how I did all that with zero knowledge of the Internet. Well, it was simple: I asked as many people as I could, who were far more clued-up than me, for help and I Googled everything! It worked, because I managed to fumble my way through.

So, I had a service to sell, a website, a Google AdWords account, and a credit card. I was ready to go...

I started with a tiny daily spending limit on my AdWords account, I tested different adverts and played around with my website (a lot). It wasn't long before I really got in the swing of things – all of a sudden I'd gone from clueless to clued-up. All of it was down to learning as much as I could and then applying what I'd learned. At times it would literally hurt my head trying to comprehend something for the first time – you know that feeling when you just don't know what you're doing?

As the months of my second year at university passed by, my business was becoming more and more profitable, and as the year drew to a close, boy was I in a different financial position than the year before! It was exciting and I really got the bug for learning.

During my final year, I decided to go to night school to learn more about web development. I'd realized how powerful the Internet was and I wanted to know more. I also wanted to get a good degree, so I recorded all my lectures on a Dictaphone and typed them up (which took me hours), so when I came to revise I would have good notes.

My third year went by quickly and I graduated with a great Law degree and a business that was doing really well. It felt good.

Now came the question, 'What shall I do now?'

I had a decision to make:

1   Do the Law Practitioners Course (LPC) and become a lawyer

2.   Keep building the business.

3.   Try and do both?!

So, I applied for the LPC and carried on building the business.

By this point I'd brought on board a business partner to help me grow it. We got a new supplier in the US, so we could unlock practically every single phone in many different countries. Then we focused on marketing.

We went all out on our SEO (search engine optimization), so that we would be number one in the organic search. We outsourced the AdWords management to a company that were experts at it and developed the website.

It was around this time that social media was taking off, so I put a blog together, set up a YouTube account, a Twitter account, a Facebook fan page, and got friendly with customers.

Things really took off...

We were receiving 100,000 hits to the website every month, selling thousands of codes, and the business ran like clockwork. But there was one big problem: I was miserable.

All my friends had jobs. I rarely met new people because I worked from home, so I became really lonely and bored.

I would constantly ask myself, 'What do you want to do? What do you like doing?'

One day I decided to volunteer at an animal rescue sanctuary! Let me tell you now... it's not the best place to meet new people!

After that I decided to become a business mentor with the Prince's Trust, which I loved, but it wasn't a great way of meeting people either.

In February of 2010 I decided I needed to do something drastic, so I went to meet my friend in Australia. Three months of meeting new people, having a good time, and not worrying about what I was going to do. It was brilliant... and then I had to come home.

All my problems were still there when I returned. It almost felt worse, because I had hoped so much that I'd have an epiphany while in Australia. I didn't. Months passed by and I felt so lost. I felt defeated and confused. I decided that the best thing for me would be to get a job.

The New Year arrived and things looked gloomy. I felt overwhelmed with negative emotions – I was really dragging myself down and I didn't know how to stop it.

Then one day it hit me: I had to take control of the situation and stop being miserable. I read a quote by Anthony Robbins that said, 'Your destiny is determined by the choices you make. Choose now. Choose well.' I realized I had to change my attitude; I had to condition myself for success. So that's exactly what I did.

I created a challenge for myself to see what would be possible – what could I create? How could I up-level my life? Would I be able to build the business and life of my dreams?

I didn't know the answers, but I was excited to find out.

I called it my 'Mission: Success Challenge,' and I was determined to go from being a confused dreamer to creating the business and life I dreamed of.

Looking back now I can see just how much this decision transformed my life.

Right then and there I decided I was going to start a project to find like-minded women who had been or were in a similar situation to me. I thought that it'd help inspire me and it would be fun. So, I put a website together and started searching online for women whose stories I could publish and that's how the Female Entrepreneur Association began.

Since then it's grown into the business of my dreams and led to me writing this book today.

For me, there's one incredibly important message I want to share and it's this:

The entrepreneurial journey is a crazy one – we come up with an idea (or often, far too many ideas!) and then we set off on our own, determined to turn our idea into a successful reality.

The emotions kick in like never before, as you're pushed outside of your comfort zone while trying to figure it all out. One moment you're ridiculously excited, inspired, and fired up. The next, you feel exhausted, drained, and unsure if you made the right choice.

Ultimately, being an entrepreneur is like being on a rollercoaster ride in the dark.

You feel alone, you feel scared, there are ups and downs, and you haven't got a clue what's coming next, but all the while you feel exhilarated. You're smiling, even though on the inside you have moments of thinking, 'What am I doing?!'

While the journey is a crazy one, there's something we all have to realize:

Success is not an accident; it's something we have to create on purpose.

And we can all do it, every single one of us.

So my challenge to you is to create your own Mission: Success Challenge and use the ideas, strategies, and tools that I share throughout the rest of this book to help you create the business and life you desire.

And just in case there's a part of you that's questioning this right now and saying, 'Yeah right, as if I'll be able to create the business and life of my dreams.'

STOP!

I know you can do it.

But, if I am wrong (which I'm not, but let's just pretend for a moment), what's the point in thinking that you can't get there? What's the point in thinking that success is not yours for the taking? That your voice is worthless? That you have no value to offer? That you have no skill or knowledge to do it?

What's the point in that?

There is no point.

It keeps you playing small.

Ultimately, we are here right now. We're living, breathing people who have incredible opportunities at our fingertips. If that doesn't scream at you, 'SPEAK UP, SHOW UP, BE AMAZING,' then I don't know what will. In this crazy and amazing universe, that quite frankly we humans don't understand, we exist here on Earth for such a limited time, so make it count, and don't listen to the people who think it's not possible.

While the journey can sometimes seem hard, it's actually simple. Success is all about doing a few things consistently. Seriously.

So let's talk about how you can show up for your business and your dreams, so that you can turn them into reality.

PART ONE

She Shows Up For Her Dreams

IT'S ALL ABOUT YOU

In 2011, when I created my Mission: Success Challenge, I knew the first thing I had to do was work on myself. I knew that I had to take 100 percent responsibility for my life, my dreams, my goals, because I was the only one who could show up for them.

In my experience, working on yourself – conditioning yourself for success – is far more important than any business strategy, because if you don't have the right mindset you'll get in your own way and won't be able to create the success you want.

So, the first step in turning your ideas into reality and becoming a wildly successful entrepreneur, is to look inward.

That's what we're going to do right now.

When I set off on my Mission: Success Challenge, one of the things I realized early on is this:

As entrepreneurs, the one thing we have to keep on doing is showing up for our dreams and our ideas, because we're the only ones that can turn them into reality.

However, the problem is that we're constantly getting in our own way. Whether it's our fears and doubts, or the fact that the people surrounding us don't think we can do it, or because we think we don't have the time or the money, or the know-how to make it happen. Whatever the challenge, we often choose to think that we can't get around it.

But, in order to succeed, we have to be prepared to push past all of the resistance –fear, overwhelm, chaos, lack of time, money, and any other obstacles that get in our way – in order to show up and say confidently, 'Hello dream, let's be a team. I'm here for you and will do all I can to put you out into the world.'

Even though we might be scared, we have to dig deep and show up.

We have to be prepared to do this right at the beginning of our entrepreneurial journey and keep on doing it, because we're forever coming up with new ideas and dreams along the way, in order to grow and flourish.

Every single part of our entrepreneurial journey will begin as an idea that will only become reality when we show up and bring it into the world.

Even writing this book was an idea that came to me one night while I was falling asleep, over four years ago now. At the beginning, I was so excited and inspired, and couldn't wait to get writing. I wanted to show up, I was trying.

But the more I got into it, the more overwhelming, confusing, and messy it became. I began to doubt myself and procrastinate. I put the book off for a year. Then, one day, I received an email from a high-powered book agent in New York, who'd read my interview with one of her clients. She loved what I was doing with FEA and was really interested in working with me to create a book.

I was ecstatic! I'd already written a lot of the book so the timing seemed perfect, and it was the kick up the backside I needed to get on with it. So I sent her all my work so far, and she said, 'Carrie, this is great, you just need to send me three expanded chapters and we'll go from there.'

'OK, I can do this!' I thought, but weeks and months rolled by, and for whatever reason, I wasn't showing up for it. I emailed her to apologize for the delay and she told me to take my time.

More months rolled by and at this point I was just embarrassed that I'd passed up such a great opportunity. I really wanted to write the book, but I kept coming up with reasons and excuses as to why I couldn't, rather than just doing it. Bottom line: I was getting in my own way.

Another year went by and while I thought about the book on a regular basis, I didn't take any action and when 2015 rolled around, I set my goals for the year and intentionally left the book off my list. I just couldn't bear another year going by having my book on my list and still not writing it, while having it constantly weighing on my mind.

But, as I often find in life, the universe was clearly paying attention and was probably thinking, 'Ha, you think you can just drop this? I don't think so!' because one morning in February, an email appeared in my inbox from the Commissioning Editor at Hay House, asking if I'd like to meet to discuss the possibility of doing a book with them.

I guess I was doing the book after all, but this time I showed up, I got out of my own way, and I took consistent action toward making this book a reality.

Life is constantly nudging all of us to play bigger, to share our messages, to turn our ideas into reality, to chase our dreams.

We were born to do great things and to dream big. If they can land men on the Moon, put robots on Mars, and fly space probes all the way to Pluto, you can achieve your dreams, and they're probably a lot closer to home. The thing is, you're the only one who can show up for them.

In life, we have so many amazing opportunities that come our way, so many dreams and ideas that we come up with, and we truly owe it to ourselves to make them happen. But so often we don't grab all the opportunities. We don't bring our ideas to life because we don't show up for them.

We dwell on all the problems, rather than concentrating on all the solutions and opportunities. We get stuck in a routine where we hold ourselves back, procrastinate, and put our dreams on hold. They stay locked inside our minds, never seeing the light of day, even though we'd really love to put them out into the world.

So what's the problem? Why do we do this?

YOU ARE YOUR BIGGEST PROBLEM

'The only thing standing between greatness and me, is me.'

WOODY ALLEN

It's not the time, the money, or any other excuse you think up. Sure, they might be valid problems, but the biggest problem you will have to overcome in order to show up for your dreams is YOU.

For such a long time, I thought my biggest problem was not having enough money to turn my ideas into reality. It was a lie, and I saw it for what it was when someone asked me, 'OK, so if I gave you $100,000 right now, what would you do with it?' The truth was, I didn't have a clue! I figured that if someone gave me that amount of money, I'd also need someone to help me to figure out what to do with it.

The truth was, money wasn't my biggest problem. I was.

Correction: The little voice in my head that would make up countless excuses and justifications for why I shouldn't do it, why I couldn't do it – that was my worst enemy. It held me back and stopped me from making progress. It stopped me from turning my ideas into reality.

The voice would scare the wits out of me. It would make me think I wasn't good enough. It would make me feel like I was stupid for even believing for a second that I could do it, that I could make my business a success or create a life that I dreamed of living. It would point out all the amazing people out there who were doing incredible things, and then it would make me feel like there was no room for me and my ideas.

We all have these voices in our head. I like to call them the 'Negative Committee.'

Do you sometimes come up with genius ideas and then think to yourself, 'I could never do that?'

I think we all do. We're so conditioned to be realistic that when we come up with amazing and crazy exciting dreams, we end up believing we can't make them a reality because they're not 'realistic.' We overthink and overcomplicate everything. We shoot ourselves down because we think our goals are out of our reach, that we don't deserve them, or that there are too many challenges in the way.

I'm here to tell you that you can achieve your goals and that you do deserve them, but first we have to stop letting two little words stand in our way...

'What if
I fall?
Oh, but
my darling,
what if
you fly?'

Erin Hanson

WHAT IF?

*'"What" and "if" are two words as non-threatening as words
can be, but put them together side by side and they have
the power to haunt you for the rest of your life.'*
LETTERS TO JULIET, SCREENPLAY BY JOSÉ RIVERA AND TIM SULLIVAN

The most common reason why our ideas stay in our head is because of two little words: 'What if?' What if it doesn't work out? What if people don't like it? What if no one buys? What if people laugh? What if I can't do this? What if I get the pricing wrong? What if it's not good enough?

The list goes on and on with reasons for why it's not a good idea to go full speed ahead toward making your ideas a reality. When you think of the 'what ifs,' you hold yourself back, overthink everything, doubt yourself, self-criticize, procrastinate, and get stuck. Then, most of the time, you end up pushing the idea to the back of your mind – it was a silly idea anyway!

But was it? Or are you just fooling yourself because you're too scared, you don't have a clue how you're going to do it and you're so caught up in the doubts that you can't see a way of figuring it out?

What if we take the 'what ifs?' and flip them on their head?

What if it's wildly successful? What if people love it? What if everyone buys it? What if people smile? What if I can do this? What if I get the pricing spot on? What if it is better than I could have ever imagined?

Things don't need to be perfect. You don't have to have it all figured out. You just have to allow yourself to move forward.

Choose to listen to and follow the voice that encourages you to move in the direction of your dreams.

THE LITTLE VOICE IN YOUR HEAD

'Your destiny is determined by the choices you make.
Choose now. Choose well.'
ANTHONY ROBBINS

The power that the little voice in our head has over our actions became clear to me when I was sitting in at a talk my friend, James Eder, was giving. As he stood on the stage, he said, 'Please can I have a volunteer?'

You could almost see the audience shrink into their seats and the room descended into an uncomfortable silence.

James said again, 'Does anyone want to volunteer?'

Eventually, a few hands went up, and one man finally got out of his seat and volunteered.

When he got to the stage, James gave him a present, thanked him for volunteering, and asked him to sit back down, while the audience applauded. Everyone seemed a little confused.

Then James said, 'My question to you is this, Why didn't you volunteer?'

The truth is, for the majority of the people in the room (me included), what stopped us from volunteering were the thoughts we were thinking, 'Oh no, what if I embarrass myself? What if I look like a fool?'

On the other hand, those that volunteered were thinking something completely different, probably along the lines of, 'Oooh, how exciting, pick me!'

This experiment had such a huge impact on me I asked James if I could use it for a TEDx talk I was giving called 'Programming Your Mind For Success.' When I got up on the stage in front of nearly 1,000 people and asked for a volunteer, the exact same thing happened – the majority of the room shrank into their seats and only one hand went up.

A guy called Ian Forrester climbed up to the stage, I handed him $20, the audience applauded and he went and sat back down. A few weeks later we met up over a cup of tea and he told me how a brush with death a few years earlier made him make the decision that he was never going to let anything stand in his way. He said, 'People are paralyzed by their fear of what might happen, and so they won't reach out and grab what's in front of them. And that's pretty much what I did.'

This small experiment proves a powerful point: What is going on inside of you (your thoughts + feelings) determines the decisions you make, and those decisions are creating your future and determining which path you're walking down.

You're the one who gets to decide whether you show up for your dreams and play big and live the life you want or whether you ignore them and play small.

It's on you.

It's all about setting out to consciously create success in your business and life every day, on purpose, no matter what.

OVERCOMING RESISTANCE: THE THREE CS

'There is no reality except the one contained within us.'

HERMANN HESSE

Ultimately, turning our ideas into reality, achieving success, living an extraordinary life, isn't reserved for a special few. Anyone can harness the power of the mind and condition themselves for success, but so often we resist following our ideas through and end up sabotaging our dreams instead.

When I've been in this situation it's felt like I'm squished up against a glass wall and my dream is calling me from the other side saying, 'Carrie, I'm over here, come on, let's get to work!' But I can't get to it. I'm stuck behind the glass wall. It's so frustrating.

This resistance is usually due to three main things or 'The Three Cs,' as I like to call them:

1. **Lack of clarity:** If you don't know what you want to make happen, how can you make it happen? You can't. You end up drifting aimlessly, not getting very far. You have to know what you're trying to achieve.

2. **Lack of confidence:** So often our fears and doubts cause us to lack confidence in ourselves and our ideas, and this holds us back from achieving what we want.

3. **Lack of competence:** Not knowing how to do what we need to do, therefore we end up procrastinating.

When we lack The Three Cs it causes so much resistance, it wreaks havoc on us mentally and emotionally, causes us to doubt ourselves ('Hello, Negative Committee, we haven't forgotten about you!'), and procrastinate. Ultimately we hold ourselves back from playing big and showing up.

I'm not just talking about the beginning of the entrepreneurial journey, but throughout it. I often go through phases of feeling stuck and not making the progress I want, but it's always due to some kind of resistance that I'm letting hold me back.

So, we have a choice to make; either:

Allow resistance to stop us achieving our dreams (mainly due to letting the Negative Committee run the show).

Or

Make the decision to overcome the resistance and not let anything stop us.

What will you do?

Choose the latter option.

Throughout my entrepreneurial journey, my Mission: Success Challenge has really helped me to overcome the resistance that's got in my way. It's helped me to move past my fears, doubts, worries, and challenges, and create the success I dreamed of.

In the following chapters I've shared different ideas for you to experiment with, as you create your own Mission: Success Challenge. Have fun with this!

CRACK YOURSELF OPEN

'When you know you're destined for greatness, your potential haunts you. It keeps you up at night. You won't feel complete until you succeed.'
MAMA ZARA

One of the biggest reasons why we fail to show up for our dreams is that we lack clarity, especially in the beginning.

My journey all started with this niggling feeling, a 'knowing' that there was somehow more. I'm sure you know just the one.

The knowing comes to us all in different ways, but it's usually an unshakable feeling that you're supposed to do something bigger with your life, something amazing.

Sometimes it's our environment and experiences that spark the knowing inside of us, like a situation that's making you feel unhappy or a challenge you're facing. Other times, it's the people around us who inspire us to want more. We see them achieving amazing things and we know deep down that we can too. It could even be a blog, a movie, a piece of music that leaves us dreaming, 'What if there's more for me?' But once we encounter our knowing, it niggles at us until we do something about it. Of course, we don't always know what's the next right step to take.

In fact, at times in my life, I've felt so unbelievably angry at my niggle/ knowing/feeling (call it what you will). This feeling of *more* abruptly enters your life, like a light switching on inside you, but then leaves you guessing as to what on earth it all means, what you're supposed to do about it, and sometimes, leaves you wanting to scream, 'What the heck am I supposed to do now?' – which ultimately leaves you feeling lost and sometimes in despair!

Recently, I was at a Gabrielle Bernstein workshop and practically everyone in the room was there because their light had been switched on, the knowing had entered their lives, but they just didn't know what they were supposed to do about it, and were there in the hope of figuring it out!

One person stood up to speak in the middle of the crowded room. Tears rolled down her face and her hands trembled, as she explained how she'd been a stay-at-home mom for five years and devoted her life to being there for other people, but her knowing had entered her life and said to her, 'What are you doing for YOU? You live for everyone else, which is amazing, but what about you? Show up for your dreams, live big.'

A light switch had gone on inside of her, she knew there was something more that she needed to be doing, but she felt so lost… and in despair. She was asking the question, 'What am I supposed to do?'

This is a question I am all too familiar with because I probably asked myself that question every day for nearly three years. The more I asked that question, the worse I felt, because I didn't have a clue!

At the time, I was running my phone unlocking business. It had become a huge success, but I felt like I was doing the wrong thing with my life. My knowing had re-entered with conviction, like it often does to steer you back on track, and it was making me question everything.

I felt like I was supposed to be doing something bigger, something more meaningful, something… I didn't bloody know. Every day, I wondered, 'Why do I feel like this? Can someone please help me?!'

There were days when I was in despair and just wanted to cry, because I didn't know what to do.

But then it dawned on me that the reason I didn't have a clue was because I was largely doing nothing.

BECOMING UNSTUCK

Until I began moving, I couldn't become unstuck, because you can't steer a parked car, and I was 100 percent parked.

So, I got committed to figuring out what my knowing was telling me and started my exploration by buying a journal. I wrote the following entry on the first page on August 27, 2008:

> 'My adventure has begun… I'm going to spend the next few months becoming independent, taking responsibility for myself, investing in myself by learning new things, and pushing myself outside my comfort zone. I'm on my journey to great success, wealth, happiness, health, peace, and wellbeing. I'm going to go through the looking glass to a life where my goals are realized. I'm so excited, nervous, and happy… I'm finally taking action.'

I didn't know what I was supposed to do in terms of a business, but I knew the kind of person I wanted to be, and I made the decision to work on being that person. I wanted to be the person who explored her passions and purpose, instead of the person I'd become – the one who stood still, overthinking everything, which then led to frequent pangs of anxiety, all because she knew she wasn't living the life she was supposed to be living.

I knew I wanted to expand, I wanted to grow, I wanted to learn, I wanted to push myself, and I wanted to see what was possible in terms of creating success, wealth, and happiness.

Really, I just wanted to explore, and over time I learned that it's OK not to have all the answers, no one does. What every person out there can do is *start*.

Start learning, start asking questions, start finding answers, start building, start growing, start becoming a better you. It doesn't matter if you don't have the answers just yet, what matters is that you *start doing*, even if it's just baby steps. Even if you only improved by 1 percent every day, within a year you would be 365 percent better.

Often, we don't really know what we're supposed to be doing, but when we take time to reflect, dig deep and explore, we know the kind of person we want to be and the kind of things we want to experience.

A mentor once told me a story of his childhood that really brought this point home to me and has stuck with me ever since.

He grew up on a social housing estate and his family was poor. When he was 12 years old, his uncle took him for lunch at the nicest restaurant he'd ever been to at that time. The waiters there treated him differently, they held the door open for him and called him sir, and for the first time in his life he realized there was more to life than he'd experienced so far.

As the years went by, he began to explore the possibility of 'more to life.' At the age of 17, while he was working as a clerical assistant at the local tax office, one of the women there said to him, 'What are you going to do with your life?'

His reply was simple: 'I'm going to be a millionaire.'

She laughed and said, 'How are you going to do that?'

He said, 'I don't know, but I am.'

That's all he knew. He didn't know how. In fact, he didn't know any of the details at all, just that there was a bigger life he needed to explore and he was going to explore it.

At 36, after lots of highs and lows, dedication and hard work, he reached his goal.

Obviously, there was a lot more to his journey, but it all began with a decision to *explore the possibilities*. He didn't know what he wanted to do, but he did know he wanted more – he wanted to be wealthy and create the life of his dreams. That decision changed his life.

So, crack yourself open and choose to live the adventure. Choose to explore the possibilities, and start by writing down and getting clear about the kind of person you want to be and the kind of things you'd like to experience.

SHE TAKES ACTION

Start a new journal today.

You might like to write on the first page, 'The entrepreneurial adventure of [*your name*]' followed by the date.

Then write your first entry and state where you're at in your life right now, what your dreams and ideas are, and the kind of life you'd love to live.

Make a commitment to yourself in writing that you're going to do all you can to follow your heart and show up for your ideas and dreams by playing big.

GIVE YOURSELF
PERMISSION TO DREAM

'Those who don't believe in magic will never find it.'
ROALD DAHL

Being an entrepreneur is a way of being. It's about dreaming big, stretching your mind to envision what's possible, what you could create, and how you could live your life.

It's about dreaming – and then doing.

When I was a teenager, I had a black folder, where I stored my ideas and dreams. Inside my folder I had a picture of a blue VW Beetle Cabriolet, with cream leather interior. I cut out a picture of my face from a photograph and stuck it over the top of the model's head. As I was still in school at the time, I also photocopied my grade card and replaced my actual grades with the ones I wanted. I altered a bank statement to show millions in my account (the balance was $36,000,000, to be precise, although I have no idea where that figure came from!). I printed out pictures of places I wanted to visit, things I wanted to buy – I even put a bottle of perfume in there of how I wanted my life to smell once I was successful.

From time to time I'd take the bottle out and just smell it and feel the feelings of success. I embodied feeling good, fulfilled, and like I was living the life I was supposed to be living. I was happy and abundant.

I created the folder for fun but really what I was doing, without truly realizing it, was conditioning my mind for success. I was planting lots of seeds about what I wanted to create for myself and how I wanted my life to be. I was getting intentional about what I thought would be amazing to have, do and experience.

I was fortunate that my dad had always encouraged me to allow space for my dreams. One year for Christmas, he bought me the CD set of the book *Ask and It is Given* by Esther and Jerry Hicks, which presents the teachings of the nonphysical entity Abraham. The book is all about learning how to manifest your desires so that you can live the joyous and fulfilling life you deserve. Dad put the CDs in a big box and wrote on the lid, 'Whatever is in the box is.' (Something that Esther and Jerry Hicks suggest doing.) He told me that whatever I put in the box I had to trust that it would find its way to me. That box became my dream box, and it still is to this day.

I often take time to dream and create goal books and goal boxes of what I want my life and business to be like. I do it for me, just to have fun. I love just exploring the exciting possibilities and stretching my mind.

SHE TAKES ACTION

When was the last time you stretched your imagination?

Maybe now's the time. Have fun and dream about what you want. You might even like to create a folder, goal box, vision board, or all of them.

There's no right or wrong way to do this. It's just about having fun and stretching your mind beyond self-imposed limitations to contemplate what's possible and to exist for a while in the knowing that perhaps it actually is.

Questions to help you get into the flow of dreaming big and stretching your mind:

- *How do you want to feel? What will help you to feel that way? Write it down or pull together pictures of things that represent what you want.*

- *What does your dream day look like?*

- *Is there anyone whose life inspires you? What specifically inspires you and what elements of their life, if any, would you like to experience in your life?*

- *What's your dream business like?*

- *What's your dream workspace?*

- *What's your dream home?*

- *What places would you love to visit?*

- *How do you want your life to be?*

- *What do you want to experience or incorporate into your life?*

- *Are there any business idols or people you'd love to meet or connect with?*

- *Anyone you'd love to work with?*

- *Do you want to write a book? If so, write it down... that's all I did :-)*

- *Do you want to give to charity? If so, which ones?*

- *How much money do you want to make and by when?*

- *How many customers, fans, followers would you like and by when?*

Go wild with this and just have fun :-)

Give yourself
permission to
dream big &
get inspired.
Magic happens
when you're
feeling inspired.

ENROLL IN THE UNIVERSITY OF OPPORTUNITY

Make the decision to enroll yourself in the University of Opportunity. This is not a university in the traditional sense of the word, rather a commitment to yourself to study opportunity: To condition your mind to see the possibilities, the potential in life. If we all did this, the world would be a very different place.

The truth is, opportunity won't come and find you, you've got to go out there and find it.

When I enrolled in the University of Opportunity I asked my dad if I could raid his book and audio collection. I'm fortunate, because my dad is someone who began his study of opportunity when he was 16 years old. The very first book he read was *Bring Out the Magic in Your Mind*, by Al Koran, and everything that he learned from that book he practiced over and over again. So, I did the same.

I began to dedicate time to learning how I could be the best version of myself, so that I could soak up the opportunities in life. I read books, listened to audio programs, went on courses, networked so that I could surround myself with people who were creating amazing opportunities for themselves. I immersed myself in the feeling that anything was possible and there was an abundance of opportunities heading my way.

When I did this, my life began to change – opportunities arose, new people came into my life. I felt so much more positive and I was making progress.

So, try it yourself and see what transformations arise for you.

SHE TAKES ACTION

What do you want to study? What will you do every day to help you open yourself to the opportunities? How will you get inspired? Write it all down and make a plan of action. You may know what's on your list already, but here are a few ideas to get you going in building your own curriculum:

- *Make a list of the books you'd love to read, and start reading the first one on your list.*

- *Reach out to any entrepreneurial friends you have and ask them for recommendations.*

- *Join relevant groups on Facebook and ask people for recommendations there too.*

MAKE THE DECISION
TO BE CURIOUS

*'In any moment of decision, the best thing you can
do is the right thing, the next best thing is the wrong
thing, and the worst thing you can do is nothing.'*
THEODORE ROOSEVELT

As you begin to explore and open up to opportunities, make the decision to be more curious and choose to let your curiosity lead you wherever it wants to take you.

I explored so many options before realizing what I wanted to do; this happens to so many of us, like one of my best friends, Ailish Lucas.

I lived with Ailish in my last year of university, and we'd sometimes chat about my business and the books I was reading. Then, she started reading the books and began to get the feeling that she was supposed to be doing more, living bigger in some way, but she had no idea what that meant… so she got curious.

When Ailish began to explore, she realized that she'd always loved beauty, so that's what she wanted to focus on, but she wasn't sure what exactly she wanted to do.

At first, the doubts crept in: 'What are you thinking going into beauty? You're too old to do this! And how will you ever make money from it? You don't even know what you want to do!'

Thankfully she ignored the doubts and, while still in her full-time job, decided to follow her heart and enrolled to train as a make-up artist and beauty therapist in her spare time.

Within a year or so she'd networked her way into the make-up artist world and was assisting on *Vanity Fair* and MTV shoots, which is very impressive to say the least.

Still, something inside her was saying, 'This isn't for you, but it's part of your journey.' So she stayed open and positive to figuring it out. Although, don't get me wrong, there were many days where she was filled with despair. She'd call me up and be so confused as to what on earth she was meant to do that it drove her crazy – like it drives the rest of us crazy.

Not long after, she decided to start a blog about organic beauty. She got everything set up and began posting, but then after a few months gave up for about a year, because of what was going on in her mind: 'Urgh, no one is coming to my site! What's the point? There are already other organic beauty bloggers, what's the point in me being one, too? This is exhausting! I don't know what I'm doing.'

She had the usual negative self-talk that a lot of entrepreneurs put themselves through. And she let it stop her.

However, her niggle to do something more grew again. It kept prodding and poking her to get back to her mission, her dreams, and her ideas. Of course, it wasn't a physical prod, it was an unshakable feeling that she needed to be studying and exploring the opportunities. She couldn't just close off from it. You can't, you'd go mad.

A while later, after losing her domain name, she started again and hasn't looked back since. (There'll be more on Ailish's story later. It's a good one!)

The point is that no one is born knowing *what they're meant to do* or goes through life knowing what they're meant to be doing *all of the time*. I often go through phases of feeling utterly confused. I'm pretty sure we all do at times, regardless of our levels of success.

Finding your way, discovering your passion, your calling, or just trying to figure out what the next big dream or idea is, isn't a walk in the park. Sometimes it feels more like a hike up a mountain and we often get stuck overanalyzing it all, rather than taking action to walk up the mountain and discover the answers.

My friend Nikki Elledge Brown took action to find her passion and purpose by creating a word of the year for herself back in 2013. Her word was 'faith,' and every morning she woke up before her husband and toddler to take some quiet time to journal, pray, and reflect – her version of the University of Opportunity (see page 27). After a week or so, she started to love waking up early and having that time for herself.

At the time she'd been writing a personal blog, and ever since she started writing it she'd received all kinds of encouraging messages of love and support from her friends and family, comments like, 'I love everything you write,' 'When are you going to write a book?' and 'You've really got a gift.'

She started to recognize these sweet comments and messages as what she calls 'divine breadcrumbs.' She realized that they had been leading her to a bigger path she was always meant to take. The messages had been championing her, encouraging her, inspiring her, and pushing her forward along her path. It was a path that scared her (because upping your game and playing bigger *is scary*), but she committed to following the trail to discover where it would lead, even though she really had no clue.

Allow yourself the space to open up and spot the 'divine breadcrumbs' in your life. We all receive them, but most of the time we don't pay attention. They're the messages, signs, and changes in our lives that tell us we are on the right path or need to realign. Sometimes it's a wise friend who can listen and share their advice. Sometimes it's just a simple email from a stranger who loves what you're doing. Other times it can just be a feeling, that what you're doing feels right.

So start paying attention. Journal, meditate, take some quiet time for yourself, learn, explore… whatever works for you, take action. Just don't do nothing.

If you do nothing, because you don't know what the right thing to do is, you'll end up drifting. Time will pass you by and you will have made no progress toward your dreams. So make the decision to be curious.

SHE TAKES ACTION

Take a moment now to get clear on how you're going to be more curious. How will you open yourself up to seeing the divine breadcrumbs?

Explore the possibilities & see where the path leads you. It's the action you take that will open your eyes & allow the clarity to unfold.

BRING YOUR VISION
INTO FOCUS

As you begin to pay more attention and open up, you'll become clearer about what it is that you need to focus on doing. With everyone I know, myself included, we all tried things that worked and got us a step closer and other things that didn't work. But ultimately, the fails also got us a step closer, because once you know what doesn't work, you can tick it off and move right past it.

Take my friend Michelle Rohr for example. She spent two years running her mom's cafe. It wasn't what she wanted to do long term, but knew it was definitely part of her journey toward figuring everything out, and the only direction she planned to go was upward. She committed to exploring and discovering what she wanted to do. She constantly moved forward, intentionally creating a life that she loved, and the cafe was another stepping-stone on her journey.

My sister, Samantha Costello, was a graphic designer for entrepreneurs and businesses before realizing that it wasn't what she wanted to do. She listened to her intuition, took notice of how she felt in her work, and then took some time to really explore, reflect, think and dig deep before deciding that she wanted to put her graphic design skills to use by creating luxury wedding stationery. Small step by small step she began down her new path.

At some point during the exploration, you too will reach a point where you have to pull your findings together and create the vision of what you want to achieve. What your dream really looks like, what excites you, what makes you passionate, and what your business mission is going to be.

So what's it to be? What's your heart and soul urging you to do? What lights you up? What's your message? What's your mission?

Getting clear on your business mission and your message is one of the most important first steps, as you'll face a lot less resistance if you know where you're going. When opportunities present themselves or there is a fork in the road, you'll be able to ask yourself, 'Does this fit with my message? Does this align with my mission?'

Back before I'd really committed to FEA, I was in my 'curious' phase, trying a variety of things to see what fitted and resonated with me. Exploring all the possibilities eventually led to me being able to get really clear on my message and mission. It was simple; I wrote down:

I want to do all I can to inspire and empower as many women as possible, to step up to their dreams, turn their ideas into reality, and build successful businesses.

I didn't know how I would do it, but I knew with every part of my being that I was going to commit myself 100 percent to my mission.

I knew after exploring for so long that this idea made my heart leap with joy, and it felt so right. It was almost a feeling of relief; in that moment I knew what I wanted to do and this then allowed me to spend my time figuring out *how* I was going to do it.

The other ideas I had at the time made me feel heavy. They felt so boring. They didn't light me up at all. Even though I could see a clear way of making money from pursuing those ideas, there was something inside that was saying, 'Nooooo, don't do it.'

I decided to go with joy, follow my passion and committed 100 percent to building the Female Entrepreneur Association.

Something that really helped me to put everything into perspective and get completely clear on what I should do, was reading a chapter in *The E-Myth Revisited* by Michael Gerber (read it, if you get a chance – it's brilliant). In his book he shares a powerful visualization exercise in which you imagine your own funeral. Attending are your friends and family, and Michael gets you to ask yourself what you want those people to be saying about the kind of life you lived, the kind of things you achieved, and the kind of person you were.

That passage of text hit me hard because I realized how precious life is. It started a fire inside of me, which made me feel like I needed to spend my life doing something I loved, doing something wonderful, having an impact, creating my dream life.

What would you want your family and friends to say about you?

SHE TAKES ACTION

What're your heart and soul urging you to do? What dream are you going to commit to showing up for?

You don't need to have it all figured out or know everything; you just need to start bringing your vision into focus.

If you've not downloaded the workbook, you can access it at http://bit.ly/SMB-Resources. Use it to help you to make a plan.

WRITE IT DOWN,
MAKE IT HAPPEN

Ever since I was a child, Dad always said to me, 'Decide what you want and write it down.'

When you take your ideas and dreams and put them on paper, all of a sudden they exist in a physical form. They're real.

In fact, since then a coach of mine, Michelle Simmonds, has always said to me, 'Write your goals down as often as you can and you'll manifest them faster.'

When you write down your goals monthly, weekly, and even daily, you constantly reaffirm where you're headed and what you want to create, and so become much more intentional about it all.

For example, for a launch I was doing for the FEA's Members' Club, I wanted to get at least 1,200 new members. This was a stretch goal, so every single day in my diary I wrote, '1,200 or more amazing women have joined the Members' Club and are loving it. They're so happy to be part of it and I'm so grateful to have them as part of it.'

Every day, I brought that goal into focus by writing it out, and every time I wrote it out it became an intentional part of my day. It became something that I thought about over and over again, and because of that, my goal turned into something much more than just a one-time idea that I'd thought about briefly. I actually ended the launch on 1,244 new (and wonderful) members.

I will admit that I have definitely not hit all of the goals I've ever set for myself, but I've come to realize that reaching them is not entirely the point. The point is that getting clear and setting goals encourages you to step up, show up more and get more intentional every day about what you're doing to support your dreams.

Even if I hadn't hit my 1,200 new members goal for the launch, I would have still grown so much, because when you get focused and intentional like that, *there's no possible way that you can't grow*.

It is also my belief and experience that when you get clear about what you want, write it down and put it out into the world, the universe has a way of manifesting it.

Take my friend Michelle for example, who recently messaged me a view of the ocean from the apartment she'd just moved into with a note saying, 'It's funny, today I realized that I had written down that I wanted to move somewhere with an ocean view and big glass doors looking out, instead of walls, with lots of breeze blowing through. Write it down and make it happen.'

SHE TAKES ACTION

Take some time now to get specific about what you want to achieve and then write it down like you've already achieved it. Just like I did above.

You could start with, 'I'm so happy now that...'

CREATE YOUR
FUTURE HISTORY

*'Use your imagination until your big dream feels so familiar
that the manifestation is the next logical step.'*

ABRAHAM HICKS

I was 10 years old when I first learned the phrase 'create your future history.' My parents had sent us – my sister, brothers, and me – on a weekend course, called 'Mindstore' with Norma and Jack Black, to learn all about positive thinking and the power of the mind.

As a child that liked to use her imagination (a lot), I loved this weekend course. We were taught tricks, like how to visualize a bell jar around you to protect yourself from people you felt were being mean or negative toward you. It was like being given super powers! My little bell jar is still on hand today when I need it to protect me, and has served me well over the years.

But the exercise I loved most was a visualization called 'The House on the Right Bank,' where you imagine walking through a field, over a river, and then picture your chosen house ahead. (When I was a child, mine was a log cabin, and it still is to this day.)

As you walk inside, there's an entrance hall and a few key rooms, each with a special purpose.

The shower room is where you can wash away any negativity. I'd stand under the shower and clap and out would pour brilliant white light to wash away stresses, doubts, and worries down the plughole.

The library is where you can ask questions and receive answers. I once used this room in a history exam at school. For the life of me, I couldn't remember the answer to one of the questions, so I closed my eyes and went to my log cabin, walked straight into the library, and pictured my history teacher, Mrs. Olsen, standing in front of me. I asked her the question and, a moment later, the answer came to me. I found out later that pretty much the exact same thing happened to my sister when she got stuck in an exam.

The bedroom is where you can set the time you want to wake up in the morning. Directly in front of a huge bed was a digital clock that took up the entire wall. As a teenager, I'd visualize going into my house, and then vividly see the time I wanted to wake up at on the wall in my bedroom. Without fail, I'd wake up bang on the time I'd set.

The conditioning gym is where you recharge your batteries. You step on a pad, press a button, and a beam of pure blue energy bathes and revitalizes your body.

The records room is where you display and store your goals and dreams. You might see pictures of places you want to go or things you want to achieve.

But the room I liked the best was the editing suite. This is your movie theatre with comfy seats and three big screens. The left screen is where you can view your past, the screen in front is where you can view your present life, and the right screen is where you can view your future. I'd get comfortable in front of the screens and visualize watching a movie of what I wanted to make happen. Then, I'd imagine actually being in the movie and I'd focus on what I could see, hear, feel, smell, and touch. I'd try to picture where I was, who I was with, and what was going on.

As a child and teenager, this was just a bit of fun, but as I got older I began to use the power of visualization more and more to help me align with my goals and manifest them. I used the practice of visualization to help me get a clearer vision of what it was that I wanted to achieve, why I wanted to achieve it and how I wanted to feel.

Back in 2012, I was nominated for The Change Makers Award, which recognized entrepreneurs under the age of 30, for my work with FEA. I was up against 26 incredible entrepreneurs, and I really wanted to win.

In the lineup were entrepreneurs who were far more successful than me and further along their journeys, but I was determined. The winner would receive a mentoring session in a helicopter with Lord Bilimoria (the founder of Cobra Beer) and a huge picture of themselves on the Coutts & Co building on the Strand in London. The winner was to be announced on stage at the MADE Festival, and even though I had no idea what the stage at the festival would look like on the day, I began to create my future history.

I asked my friend, Jason Jackman, to record a guided visualization for me called, 'Programming Your Mind For Success.' In this 15-minute audio Jason guided me into a deep altered state, so I felt very relaxed, and then he began to make suggestions about creating the success I wanted. He shared powerful success affirmations and allowed me to create a movie in my mind where I envisioned what I wanted to make happen.

I listened to it every single day and vividly visualized standing on the stage with the other nominees and hearing someone announce, 'And the winner is Carrie Green!'

The crowd cheered, I felt complete elation, and then I got in the helicopter with Lord Bilimoria. I actually imagined a particular moment where I was looking out of the window and thinking, 'You visualized being here, and you knew you would do it.'

I had conversations in my head with Lord Bilimoria that were so detailed and vivid I felt like I'd already met him.

The festival finally rolled around. All of the nominees were taken up onto the stage, and as I stood there, it was like I'd already been there before because I'd visualized and imagined it for so long. As it happened, the person announcing the winner was none other than HRH The Duke of York! We all stood there, waiting patiently for him to announce the winner, and then he said, 'And the winner is Carrie Green!' I was elated, excited, and so ridiculously happy that my visualization had become my reality.

I can no longer really distinguish between what I visualized beforehand and what actually happened on the day, because they seem to have merged into one. And who honestly knows, maybe winning had nothing to do with my visualizations, but I've had too many weird coincidences happen not to believe that there's at least something to it all.

Science agrees and a number of studies, described in 'Seeing is Believing' published in *Psychology Today* (Dec 2009) demonstrate just how powerful visualization can be in shaping our destiny because 'thoughts produce the same mental instructions as actions.'

This phenomenon is thanks to neuroplasticity – the ability of the brain to continuously create new neural pathways. When we repeat a skill that we are trying to master, we strengthen the neural networks that represent that action. The same thing happens in our brains, whether we perform the action, or just visualize it.

Your brain literally can't tell the difference between an action you performed and an action you visualized.

So make the most of it and take time to visualize achieving what you want.

This works, and I know I'm not the only one who has used visualization to create their future history. I know a lot of entrepreneurs who use visualizations to help them create business success. Also, most athletes train in visualization too.

Muhammad Ali, in particular, was famous for his accurate future histories. In 1962, he publicly predicted that he would win the fight against veteran boxer Archie Moore. Ali said, 'Archie Moore will fall in four,' meaning round four of 12. Moore responded saying he had perfected a new punch called 'The Lip-Buttoner,' which was a dig that Ali should shut his mouth.

Sure enough, Ali beat Moore with a knockout in the fourth round.

This wasn't the only time that Ali predicted the defeat of an opponent, down to the exact round, and he attributed this to a powerful visualization technique called, 'future history.'

Prior to a fight, Ali would visualize progressing through the whole event and see himself at the end, with his arms raised in the air and the referee proclaiming him the champion. He would visualize this so vividly, with total commitment and belief. He would hear the crowds cheering and shouting his name. He would feel how amazing it felt to win. He was totally in the zone. All his energy and focus would then be directed to making this happen. He would immerse himself in his imagination and experience the fight over and over again.

When he walked into the ring, he was extremely well prepared, both mentally and physically. He'd already won the fight in his mind and so his subconscious would be constantly looking out for ways to make his desired outcome true.

Visualization is kind of magical, but on the other hand it makes total sense, because the fact is we're all using the power of our minds to conjure up our future, it's just that most people aren't aware they're doing it and don't get intentional about what they're creating.

So get intentional about it and use it to your advantage. There's a 12-step process at the end of this chapter you can use to help you.

When you use your mind to cultivate the stories of what you do want — rather than what you don't want — and actively feel the feeling of what you want to create, weird and wonderful things will start happening.

Of course, visualizing a successful outcome doesn't always come easily and there are times when I really struggle to do it. Sometimes I sit down to visualize and I just don't know what to visualize. All of my goals and dreams seem scattered and I can't get my mind to focus on anything.

At one time, this kept happening to me so I spent some time figuring out a way to overcome it.

I ended up taking time to write out everything I wanted to achieve on little pieces of paper and then folding them all up and putting them into a jar. I called it my 'Dream Jar.'

I decided that I was going to pick a piece of paper out of my jar three times a day, set a timer on my phone for two minutes, and take time to immerse myself in experiencing having what was on the piece of paper, by vividly visualizing it happening.

Doing it this way meant that I could get very clear about what I was going to be visualizing – I didn't feel scattered and unfocused.

I found that with the goals I'd written down that I'd never visualized happening before, I had to get clarity around my goal before I started to visualize it happening. I also found that the more I visualized a goal, the more intense and detailed the visualization became – it evolved. In the first few days of visualizing something new, everything seemed hazy in my mind, but as I kept on visualizing it the image became clearer and clearer.

For example, I have a goal to meet and be interviewed by Oprah Winfrey and when I first began visualizing this happening I would imagine being sat with her on a sofa, with the audience in front of me and in my head I would be thinking, 'I can't believe I'm finally here, I've visualized this happening so many times.' And then the more often I visualized it, the more detailed the image became. I imagined what it would feel like to shake her hand and how it would feel to hug her and what she would say to me and what I would say to her… until in my mind I was having a full-blown conversation with her.

I've yet to meet Oprah, but I know I want to, so I'm going to do all I can to focus my energy on meeting her. Plus, visualizing meeting Oprah is fun!

So create your Dream Jar, get strengthening your visualization muscles, and have fun creating your future history. Just as clearly as you can imagine something you've experienced in the past, you can imagine something that you want to happen in your future.

Start creating your own success on purpose now.

SHE TAKES ACTION

Get intentional and stay intentional by using this 12-step visualization process to create your future history. If you can, make time to visualize achieving what you want at least once a day. All you need to do is:

1. *Think of the outcome you desire. What do you want to experience or achieve?*

2. *Take some time to visualize the outcome happening with total belief.*

3. *See yourself in the picture – what do you look like?*

4. *What can you hear?*

5. *What do you feel?*

6. *What can you see around you? See it.*

7. *What can you touch? Touch it.*

8. *Change your posture to how it would be in your imagination.*

9. *Make the image bigger.*

10. *Make the image brighter.*

11. *Make the sounds louder.*

12. *Intensify the feeling. Truly experience what you want, like it's really happening.*

CREATING YOUR DREAM JAR

Write out everything you want to achieve on little pieces of paper and then fold them all up and put them into a jar – this is your Dream Jar.

Pick a piece of paper out of your jar every day. (I try to do this every morning and evening, my friend told me she does it while she cleans her teeth – so do whatever works best for you.) Set a timer on your phone for two minutes, close your eyes, and immerse yourself in experiencing achieving the goal written on the piece of paper, by vividly visualizing it happening.

HELLO, GOOGLE

Once you experience the excitement that comes from intentionally creating your future history, you'll feel inspired and eager to get started with turning your idea into reality.

The next step is to figure out how you're going to make it happen.

When I started my first business, I had zero idea what I was doing. I knew nothing about building an online business. In fact, even later, when I was setting up the Female Entrepreneur Association or starting my magazine or my membership site, I still had no idea how to do it. None.

So I said, 'Hello' to Google.

My dad always used to say, 'There's no such word as "can't". I know how to do it, and when I show you how, you'll be able to do it too, because if one person can, we all can.'

None of us have all the answers, and at the beginning of a new idea we tend to have rather few, but the answers are out there somewhere and it's up to us to find them.

How do you find them? Well, I'd start with Google. I've practically learned to build all of my businesses thanks to Google and the Internet. I also learned some amazing things along the way from people I've met, too, but even most of those connections came about through the Internet! So all in all, pretty much all of my knowledge has come through Googling, YouTubing, and asking questions in forums. There is a wealth of knowledge out there that's waiting for us to tap into it. So tap in.

SHE TAKES ACTION

We'll talk more about the specifics of setting up an online business in Part 2, but for now, make a list of the things you need to learn and the skills you need to develop. Then, get on Google and discover what people, websites, videos, books, programs can help you.

THE DOUBTS
CREEP BACK IN

'Watch your thoughts, for they become words. Watch your words,
for they become actions. Watch your actions, for they become
character. Watch your character, for it becomes your destiny.'

FRANK OUTLAW

As I began Googling, I realized how little I actually knew. I was prepared to take more steps to show up for my dreams, but I noticed myself beginning to doubt everything. There's a lot of information out there and a lot of people doing amazing things, and it's easy to develop impostor syndrome.

This is exactly what happened to Nikki. She set off on her journey, got clear on her idea, began to Google, and then the doubts kicked in. She said to me:

'I was thinking, I know I want to be able to help people with communication, but it seems like everybody out here has a certificate of some kind. Do I need a coaching certificate to help people with communication? What am I supposed to have? I was totally doubting my qualifications. Never mind the almost 2,000 hours of college-level teaching experience, the Master's degree with a 4.0, and the decade

of experience studying communication. I was still wondering, WAIT. Am I ready? Is this really something I can do?'

Nikki shared her doubts on a popular blog for female entrepreneurs, and the blog owner (now a dear friend of hers) replied back with the exact message that Nikki (and so many of us) needed to hear: 'You are absolutely qualified.'

That simple bit of encouragement from a complete stranger was all Nikki needed to make her realize that she really could do it.

Often it's when we start exploring our ideas more deeply that the Negative Committee chime in and whisper things like, 'You're not good enough to do it! Who do you think you are? Are you serious? You don't have the time, money or skills for this! You aren't qualified!'

This is why for me a big part of my Mission: Success Challenge was (and still is) about conditioning myself for success and learning how to get a grip of what is going on inside my mind.

I've learned some amazing strategies that have really helped me to take control of my thoughts and move past the resistance, so over the next few chapters I want to share those strategies with you.

WATCH YOUR THOUGHTS

I realized that the first step in taking control of what was going on in my mind was to *know* exactly what was actually going on in my mind, so, over the course of a few days, I kept a note of my thoughts throughout the day.

I discovered that when I was being productive and making great progress, the thoughts I was thinking were positive and I was feeling good. But when I was being really unproductive, my thoughts tended to be things like, 'I can't be bothered,' 'I don't know how,' and 'I can't do this.'

The thing is, we all think these things from time to time, and that's fine. The problem arises when we're not checking in with ourselves and we're allowing these thoughts to carry us through the day and determine the decisions we make.

So check in with yourself and pay attention to what's really going on.

SHE TAKES ACTION

When you wake up in the morning, write down what you're thinking and feeling. Then set an alarm for every hour during the day. When the alarm goes off, stop and write down what you're thinking and feeling. Finally, when you go to bed, write down your thoughts and feelings again.

Use this exercise whenever you're feeling stuck and not making the progress you want, when you're not showing up for your dreams, and use it when you want to tune in with yourself and find out what's going on internally.

It's so powerful! Definitely give it a try and see what comes up for you.

'If you think you're too small to be effective, you've never been in bed with a mosquito.'

Betty Reese

BE WILLING TO CHOOSE
DIFFERENT THOUGHTS

"'I AM," two of the most powerful words. For what
you put after them shapes your reality.'
BEVAN LEE

Becoming more aware of your thoughts is empowering because then you can do something about them. You can actually change your thoughts.

William James once said, 'The greatest discovery of my generation is that human beings can alter their lives by altering their attitudes of mind.'

I realized that being willing to change was a massive step toward conditioning myself for success. I was opening myself up to something better.

Whenever I caught myself thinking negatively, I stopped myself by literally saying, 'Stop,' really firmly. Then, I was willing to see things differently. I knew I had to change my perspective and question my doubts. I had to look through them and see the light on the other side, so that I could get past them.

I definitely had some deep-rooted issues that would bubble up over and over again, thoughts like, 'Who am I to do this?' I'll admit that they were hard to break down. But I just kept practicing saying 'Stop' and forcing myself to feel positive by thinking of something good and, over time, started to weaken the connection I had with the negative thoughts, until one day I realized that they didn't bother me anymore at all. I had the strength to move past them easily.

Ultimately, we get to choose to let go of our thoughts.

Oprah made a powerful point about this in a story she shared in a video I watched.

She described an exercise in which her yogi asked her to lie down and close her eyes. He then listed different objects and asked her to let them appear before her mind and then let them go: 'A full moon. An oak tree by the bank of a river. A red triangle.'

What she learned from this exercise was that the observer of the red triangle, the oak tree, and the full moon was the same observer who observes all of the thoughts that come in and out of the mind, all day long.

The point is this – you have the same control of the thoughts that are coming into your mind and keeping you stuck. You can let them go, too.

SHE TAKES ACTION

Over the next few days, whenever you notice yourself feeling low or having negative thoughts – whether it's feeling panicky due to a lack of time/money or feeling low because everything seems impossible – take control of them. Say, 'Stop' out loud, really firmly to yourself, and then let the thought go and think about something else – anything else! Remember, that you can let them go, just as easily as you can let go the thought of a red triangle :-)

MAKE FRIENDS WITH DISCOMFORT

'For a star to be born there's one thing that must happen: a gaseous nebula must collapse. So collapse. Crumble. This is not your destruction. This is your birth.'

N.T.

Everyone who is trying to turn their ideas into reality and build a successful business feels discomfort at some stage. We're all pushing ourselves to do things we've never done before, and that causes the resistance to rise up – the fears, the doubts, the worries – and it feels uncomfortable.

Just know that this discomfort is not your destruction, it is your birth.

It means you're on your way to achieving greatness. So whenever you feel it bubbling up I want you to say:

'Bring it on, discomfort. I knew I'd meet you here, and I'm ready for you. Actually, I'm excited that you've arrived because it means I'm moving in the direction of my dreams. I'm going to keep on climbing up, up, up, so let's be friends, yes?'

Give yourself permission to feel comfortable with being uncomfortable. Know that it is part of the journey and that it is helping you to grow.

It's most definitely easier said than done when you're in the thick of it! Which is why you'll need to have a few tricks up your sleeve to help you stay positive – even when you're unsure of everything. Here follow some of my favorites.

Start with your body

I learned from Tony Robbins that the fastest way to change how you feel is to change your posture (Easy enough!). Usually, when we're feeling low or overwhelmed or out of control we're hunched over, with head held low. When we're feeling positive and confident then we tend to sit or stand straight, head held high.

Changing your posture to standing or sitting tall, with your head high, psychologically tells your brain that you're feeling good. It changes your state of mind. Whenever you become aware that you are feeling low or stressed or frustrated, take a deep breath and smile. Smiling has the power to make you feel so much better in an instant, and change your posture to one that exudes confidence.

As the saying goes, 'fake it until you make it.' This is a bit of trickery, after all.

Feed your mind

I was having a conversation once with Michelle about entrepreneurial things, like dealing with the tough times, and she said to me, 'You can't feel negative or down when you have Tony Robbins in your ears.'

I happen to agree with her.

When Michelle first started exploring her entrepreneurial niggle she went through a two-year phase of feeling pretty miserable. Even though she was on her journey, she wasn't yet doing what she wanted to be doing.

She'd quit college, knowing that she was supposed to be doing something bigger, and headed home to Guam. As I mentioned earlier in the book, Michelle wanted to start her own business, but ended up working full-time in the family coffee shop and quickly became consumed with juggling a dozen plates – literally and figuratively! It was a huge learning experience, but she learned what kind of business she didn't want to build. She wasn't doing things the way she would have liked and she wasn't running her dream business.

Still, she knew she was on her journey and so she honored the process, because she knew the only direction she was going was upward (even though it might not have felt like it at times).

To help her navigate her way, she began to feed her mind with personal development. Every single day, while driving to the cafe, she would listen to *Success Magazine* on CD – and some she'd listen to over and over again. While she was at work, serving the customers, she had one headphone in, and all day long she'd be listening to podcasts by motivational speakers such as Tony Robbins and Jack Canfield.

Every day, she was feeding her mind information that was helping her to move forward. She was 100 percent committed to consuming information that would help her mind to get to a different place, a place where she felt like she was growing, a place where she felt like things were possible.

By conditioning herself in this way, she never gave herself a chance to go backward, as all of her energy and focus was being directed forward.

When I kicked off my Mission: Success Challenge, I listened to a lot of motivational audio programs, and still love to discover new amazing audio programs, podcasts, books, and videos that will help me to train my brain to feel positive.

In fact, for a few years every week I posted an inspirational video from YouTube to my website and called the post 'Motivation Monday,' so if you want to start your inspirational playlist, that blog series is a great place to start – you can find them at http://bit.ly/SMB-Resources

Words are powerful. The right ones can change our lives, how we think and the decisions we make.

SHE TAKES ACTION

Make it your mission to feed your mind with amazing words consistently.

Take some time to research great audio programs or books you want to read, browse through the podcasts at iTunes, or head over to YouTube and create a playlist of inspirational videos you can watch time and time again. Make it easy on yourself by having the right stuff at your fingertips, as and when you need to call on it.

Create your inspirational music playlist

Another thing that can be useful to keep on hand is a music playlist. Mine is a compilation of songs that make me feel inspired, fired up, and happy. Whenever I listen to them, I feel like my mind is being conditioned for success. I instantly feel more confident and start thinking things like, 'Come on Carrie, you can do this, you know you've got it!'

I sometimes wake up in the morning, put on my music, and dance around like an idiot to make myself feel fired up and inspired and ready to make amazing things happen.

Music is powerful. It evokes so many feelings inside of us, so use it to your advantage.

SHE TAKES ACTION

What songs inspire and fire you up? Create an inspirational playlist and listen to them.

Pick a word

I mentioned earlier how Nikki decided to pick a word for the year back in 2013. Her word was 'faith,' and she made the decision to focus her energy on it (see page 31).

Words are so powerful, when we pick one that means a lot to us and use it to keep us moving in the right direction, miraculous things can start to happen.

In 2012, I was a year into running FEA, and while things were going well and everything was growing, I was struggling because it wasn't financially sustainable in any way, shape, or form. This would often send me into a panic and I can't tell you how many times I thought, 'Carrie, go and get a job, and put yourself out of your misery!'

Instead, I chose to TRUST.

'Trust' became my word – fierce trust that I was exactly where I needed to be, that I was moving in the right direction, and that everything would work out as it was supposed to – even though I didn't know whether it would.

I designed a little graphic of the word trust, printed it out, and stuck it on my wall, so I constantly reminded myself to trust the process.

To this day, 'trust' remains one of my big words. I rely on it all the time. In fact, while writing this book, I've had to lean on it so much and just remember to trust that everything will work out as it's supposed to.

Over the years, I've formed attachments to other words and used them when I've needed them.

In 2015 things with FEA were going amazingly well, but my goal was to breakthrough and up-level my business. In order to do that, I needed courage to play a bigger game, I knew I had to be bold and dare to shine more. I picked 'courage' as my word, and set my intentions of embodying it.

Again, I created a graphic, printed it off, and developed an attachment to it. Whenever I felt out of my depth and wanted to back off and hide, I leaned on my word to push me on.

There was another time when I realized that I'd been working so hard on FEA that I'd forgotten to have fun and enjoy myself, so I chose to focus on the word 'fun,' and I intentionally pulled fun into my world. I made the decision to go on more vacations and to do more things that would help me to enjoy life more.

SHE TAKES ACTION

What's your word? Write it down. Create a graphic and stick it on your wall where you'll see it every day.

I also have my inspirational words, quotes, and affirmations all over the place — on my walls, on my phone, on my laptop screensaver — positive suggestions everywhere! But my favorite quote of all is, 'I can and I will. Watch me.' It never fails to make that empowering voice inside of me speak up louder and say, 'You can do this.'

What's your quote?

BE GRATEFUL FOR WHAT YOU HAVE

*'Be thankful for what you have; you'll end up
having more. If you concentrate on what you
don't have, you will never, ever have enough.'*
OPRAH WINFREY

A few years ago I discovered that life gets so much better when we
focus on what we're grateful for. At the time I was seriously stressed
out because, like most entrepreneurs, I was trying to spin far too many
plates, I wasn't where I wanted to be (are we ever?!) and where I did
actually want to be felt impossible to reach. I ended up focusing so much
on feeling like I was a million miles away from reaching my goals.

Then I came across a video on YouTube of Zig Ziglar talking about the
'attitude of gratitude.' In the video he was telling the story of a woman
who was complaining about her job, so he asked her to get out her
notepad and write down all the reasons why she liked her job. By the
end of it, her perspective had completely changed. Instead of feeling
frustrated and angry about the things that she didn't like about it, she
now felt happy and positive about all the things she did like. She had an
'attitude of gratitude.'

So I sat down with a notepad and pen and began writing out all of the things I was grateful for in my business and life. The more I wrote, the more things I came up with. When I'd eventually run out of things to write I took a deep breath, looked at my list and smiled. Everything was OK, more than OK in fact! Things were wonderful, it was just that I'd been so blinded by focusing on the negatives that I'd lost sight of the positives.

Even things like the fact I could see the trees in the garden, swaying in the wind, and appreciating the fact I had a laptop and Internet connection that were enabling me to learn, grow, and build my business. These were things I'd been overlooking every single day, so I decided from that moment on I was going to live with an attitude of gratitude instead.

Every day I began making a conscious effort to think of three things I was most grateful for – whether it was a smile from a stranger, something one of my team did, or simply the fact I exist. I would spend a minute or two really feeling the gratitude in the pit of my stomach. When I started to do this I noticed a shift in my life, I felt happier and life flowed better, because I was focusing more on the positives and so ultimately, more of the positives began to flow back into my life.

SHE TAKES ACTION

Get a notepad and write down all of the things you're grateful for right now and stick that list somewhere you can see it every day.

Then when you wake up think of three things you're grateful for, throughout the day remind yourself of what you're grateful for, and list three more things at night before you go to bed.

When you think about these things, really feel them and connect with them. If someone did something kind for you, think of how it made you feel and just create that feeling inside yourself again.

BELIEVE MORE

'Many people limit themselves to what they think they can do. You can go as far as your mind lets you. What you believe, remember you can achieve.'
MARY KAY ASH

I once read an incredible story about the power of self-belief that amazed me so much I got goose bumps while reading it.

Wilma Rudolph was born prematurely in 1940, weighing just 4½lbs. Not long after that, she was struck down by polio, which caused infantile paralysis, and a number of serious childhood illnesses. The doctors said it was a miracle that she was alive but would never be able to walk properly. Wilma believed something different.

At the age of 11, Wilma walked for the first time without her leg brace. At 12, she was playing basketball with her brothers and sisters. At 13, she began to run. At 14, she began to run really fast! At 15, she was extraordinary. Wilma Rudolph went on to become the fastest woman on the planet, winning three gold medals at the 1960 Olympics.

Now that is the power of self-belief.

Anything is possible when you put your mind to it. Believe that what you want is yours for the taking.

They thought it was impossible for a human being to run a mile in under four minutes. Well, we all now know that it is possible thanks to Roger Bannister, who believed when everyone else didn't.

They thought it was impossible for a human to travel at the speed of sound, but Felix Baumgartner smashed that belief in 2012.

People are doing the impossible every day. Will you be one of them? Are you prepared to stand out from the crowd and believe that you can achieve things, even though some might think it's impossible or unrealistic?

Too often, we limit ourselves by thoughts of self-doubt, choosing to believe it's impossible for us to achieve great things, as others have. The fact is, those thoughts destroy your chances of success. If you limit what is possible, then you will never achieve the things you want.

SHE TAKES ACTION

Use the following affirmation to help power your self-belief:

'Success begins with me. Success is inside me, and it's something I have to create on purpose, day in, day out.'

Write it out and pin it on your desktop, on the dashboard of your car – wherever you'll see it regularly. The more you do it, the more automatic it'll become, like riding a bike or driving a car.

Just believe that you can.

'Nothing is impossible. The word itself says "I'm Possible."

Audrey Hepburn

ASK THE UNIVERSE
FOR IT

Throughout my entire entrepreneurial journey, I've always asked the universe for help. In fact, when I was a teenager my dad bought me a book called *The Cosmic Ordering Service* by Barbel Mohr, who suggests you literally place an order with the universe by telling it what you want, then imagine it happening. At the time, I thought it was a fun little concept to experiment with. Whenever I needed a parking space in a busy area, I would cosmic order a space by saying in my head, 'I cosmic order the best car parking space to be available when I arrive.' Then I would visualize a space being available for me. It works every time.

Whenever I'd lost something, I would cosmic order to find it. Often within the hour I would have found it. In fact, I actually did this recently when I'd lost a necklace; after I'd cosmic ordered to find it I decided to go into my bedroom, lift up my bed and there was my necklace. It never fails to amaze me!

Essentially, all I'm doing is asking the universe (call it what you will) for guidance. Not only do I do this in my personal life, I do it in business all the time.

Back in 2012 I came up with the idea to create a digital magazine for women in business; people thought I was a little crazy for wanting to do this, I mean I had no experience. I had no team. Heck, I had hardly any money to invest. From an outsider's perspective, I could see why they thought I was a little insane.

But I believed in my idea and I gave myself permission to step up my game and reach out to people who were way more established and successful than me for an interview. Then I asked the universe for help. I did this by sitting down and writing out a wish list of people I wanted to interview for the cover. When I wrote out that wish list of people, I was sending a message out to the universe saying, 'I would love to interview these wonderful people for my magazine, and I know you can work magic, so please can you work some magic for me? Thank you.'

With the wish list I'd created, I found that the interviews came about in the most mysterious of ways.

For Issue 2, I wanted to feature Lady Michelle Mone, founder of Ultimo. I had no idea how I was going to reach her, it wasn't like I could just drop her an email. So I placed my cosmic order and started visualizing her photo on the cover, and within a few days received an email from my bank manager, Gemma, inviting me to be her guest at an upcoming event, where Michelle Mone was the keynote speaker.

I knew full well that at these types of events you rarely get to meet, let alone have a conversation with the keynote speaker, but I'd asked the universe, and here was my sign.

So, along I went to the event, and sure enough Michelle was actually attending the event, too. She was sat at a table up at the front, so after she'd finished her talk, I made my way over to her, introduced myself, told her how much I admired her and asked if it would be possible to interview her. She said yes and gave me the contact details for her assistant. A couple of weeks later, the interview was sorted.

For Issue 4, I wanted to interview Jessica Herrin, founder and CEO of Stella & Dot. That very same week, I received an email from them saying that Jessica was going to be over for an event in the UK, and I went along and interviewed her.

For Issue 5, I wanted to interview Michael Gerber, *New York Times* bestselling author of a book that had changed my life (see page 36). I began to reach out by emailing and calling the number on his website, but got no response. About a week later, as I was sat there trying to figure out how to make it happen, an idea popped into my head to go and check out his Facebook fan page.

There I was, on his fan page, and right in front of me was an image of an inspirational graphic that my brother had created for FEA. It was right there, at that exact moment!

I went to my fan page to double-check it was the same one, and then my brother posted a comment saying he'd created it for FEA. Then, I left a comment saying, 'We are flattered that you like it :) maybe you'll let us interview you for our magazine?'

They messaged back with an email address, and a week or so later I was having a phone call with Michael E. Gerber. It was amazing.

So many weird and wonderful things like that have happened throughout my journey. Is it really the universe helping? Who knows! But, from my experience, something magical happens when you ask.

In fact, the actor Jim Carrey summed it up well in a commencement speech he gave to Maharishi University of Management class of 2014:

'So many of us choose our path out of fear disguised as practicality. What we really want seems impossibly out of reach and ridiculous to expect, so we never dare to ask the universe for it. I'm saying that you can ask the universe for it.'

Dare to ask.

SHE TAKES ACTION

What would you like help with or answers to at the moment?

Ask the universe for help, ask for a sign and trust that you'll get it.

IT'S ALL JUST
AN EXPERIMENT

'Eventually all the pieces fall into place. Until then, laugh at the confusion, live for the moment and know that everything happens for a reason.'
SEX AND THE CITY, CANDACE BUSHNELL

Ultimately, there are many ways to condition yourself for success. You can meditate, do affirmations, visualizations, pay attention to what's going on inside… the list goes on and on.

But we're all different. What works for me might not work for you. I love doing visualizations, but you might hate it. That's OK. Just explore the options, and do whatever appeals to you most. When you find something that works well for you, create an intentional daily practice for it. Make sure it's part of your own Mission: Success Challenge.

When I started FEA, I set off knowing that it was one big experiment. I wanted to see how many women I could help and inspire. I wanted to see how far I could share my message. I wanted to see what I could create.

There were no guarantees for how things would work out, even though I believed (most of the time) that somehow something wonderful was going to happen. So I just had to view it all as a bit of a fun experiment.

Don't get me wrong, I was intending for it to be incredibly successful, but in order to navigate the entrepreneurial journey and enjoy it as much as possible, I needed to just let go and allow it to be all about testing, trying, exploring, learning, and seeing how it all unfolded. Because you can never really know how it will work out.

When I started FEA, I had no idea I would create a magazine at some point and interview my idols. I had no idea that I would create a membership site and have over 3,000 members within the first two years. I didn't know that stuff yet, so I just had to keep on experimenting, keep on conditioning myself for success, keep on trusting the process, and keep on becoming the person I needed to be in order to show up for my dreams and play big.

That's all.

We can all do it. We can all show up for our dreams, no matter how scary it is. We can all become the people we need to be in order to become wildly successful entrepreneurs.

We just have to choose our dreams over our fears.

It's time to step up and play the game of business and life bigger than ever before.

So, now let's talk about how you can make your dreams and ideas a successful reality.

The world is ready and waiting for you. YOU'VE GOT THIS.

• THE CHECKLIST •

She Shows Up for Her Dreams

Here's your checklist to help you condition yourself for success and show up for your dreams.

O   Make the decision to create your own Mission: Success Challenge. Open yourself up to the possibilities! What amazing things could you achieve?

O   Be curious in the pursuit of following your dreams and creating a successful business.

O   Start a journal of your entrepreneurial adventure. Write in it daily (if you can) and share what's been happening, what you're trying to achieve, how you've been feeling – get it all out, it's eye-opening and therapeutic!

O   Allow yourself to start dreaming big and getting clear about what you actually want, what success means for you.

O   Visualize your future history daily – see it happening, feel it happening, believe that it will happen.

O   Pay attention to your thoughts in the morning, throughout the day, and at night – choose empowering thoughts.

O   Change your posture to change your state and feel good.

O   Create a list of books, videos and programs you want to check out to help you flourish and grow.

O   Create your inspirational music playlist and listen to the songs that help you to feel good.

O   Choose your word or statement for the year and make a commitment to live by it. Write it down and place it where you'll see it daily.

O   Think about what you're grateful for at least once a day.

O   Get the universe on your side and ask her to bring what you need.

O   Write out your favorite affirmations and quotes and place them around your home and workspace, where you'll see them every day. Put positive suggestions everywhere!

O   Be prepared to experiment with your ideas.

Choose your dreams over your fears.

PART TWO

She
Gets Herself
Out There
To Shine

LET'S TALK BUSINESS

In 2015, after running her latest business for just over nine months, Kimra Luna made over $880,000 in revenue. This did not happen by accident. It happened very much on purpose, and her journey began years before with a voice inside that whispered, 'There's something more.'

A few years earlier, she had been living in California at her in-laws' house, with her husband and their three-year-old son. They'd been relying on food stamps and government assistance for the previous four years. A few months later, she gave birth to her second son, and on the same day her husband's minimum wage temp job ended.

Sat there with her new baby in her arms, she was wondering how she could give her kids the great life they deserved when she had nothing to her name.

Despite the situation, Kimra and her husband remained positive. They'd been studying personal development for years, setting their intentions with the universe, and attempting to manifest what their hearts desired.

Then, the universe started to answer back. Kimra's husband managed to get a job in North Dakota as a FedEx parcel carrier, and after six months of being apart, they had enough money saved up for Kimra and their two boys to move out. Her husband was transferred to Virginia and they were all together again – in a new apartment and finally off welfare. Things were looking up.

Another six months passed by, and Kimra was beginning to feel bored by being a stay-at-home mom. She told her husband that she wanted to invest in an iMac with their tax refund and get the Internet connected, so she could start a blog and make some money on the side.

She quickly became obsessed with online marketing. She was learning all she could by attending webinars, listening to podcasts, and reading books. In January 2014, she made a commitment to herself to start a business and make $5,000 per month.

As they had no money, she decided to take out a credit card with a spending limit of $3,000, and she used it to get the ball rolling.

The first thing she did was enroll in an online business course to help her lay the foundations and figure out what she would do. When class began in March, she devoted herself to becoming the best student ever because she knew that if she kept her goal in the front of her mind, she'd manifest $5,000 a month with no problem at all.

After opening herself up to exploring the possibilities, she decided that she'd be good at teaching others the skills she'd learned, and so on May 5, 2014, she launched her website – it wasn't perfect, but she was ready to get it out there.

A week later, she ran her first ever webinar, teaching people about PicMonkey. She had nothing to sell, but she had a lot of knowledge and value to give. Shortly after that, she put together her first paid course, all about using Facebook Ads, and she made her first sale.

Kimra was causing a stir online, by being so present in Facebook groups, adding so much value, and by building relationships with people within the communities. It wasn't long before people were coming to her to ask for more help with what she was teaching. So, she decided to put together a 12-week one-on-one program to teach people everything she'd learned. She threw a sales page together, decided to charge $2,000 and then waited to see what would happen.

That day, three people signed up, and within six weeks she'd made over $10,000. It was phenomenal.

She kept listening for ways to help the entrepreneurs around her, and she began to run more tailored webinars to address the specific problems she could see her audience struggling with. She gave away hours of free, in-depth trainings, and all she was focused on was delivering really simple, straightforward, solution-centered training that literally anyone could follow.

By July, Kimra was doing so well that her husband was able to retire from his full-time job, so he could spend more time with his family and do the things he loved.

As more time passed by, Kimra began to realize that she could package up everything she'd learned and had been teaching into an online program. In August 2014, she launched Be True Brand You. When the doors to the launch closed, after three and a half weeks, she'd made $64,000 in sales.

Throughout the rest of the year, she kept adding value, kept getting herself out there, kept building her audience and her email list. When she did another launch in February 2015 she made $721,200 in revenue.

Not too shabby ;-)

Let's break down Kimra's success:

- She invested in her own personal development and got into the habit of asking the universe for what she desired.

- She allowed herself to explore the possibilities.

- She got clear on what she wanted and committed to it.

- She took a calculated risk to invest in learning all she could to create the success she wanted.

- She decided to be the best student ever.

- She leveraged the Internet to get herself out there and built her platform (creating a website, doing webinars, networking online, etc.) even though things weren't perfect.

- She got clear on who her audience were and then focused on serving them the best she could.

- She listened and paid attention to her audience's needs and catered to them.

- She created products that she knew they wanted.

- She kept going and going and going – learning, creating, serving, and growing the whole time.

Her success is not an accident. She's created it so intentionally.

You see, Kimra was showing up for her dreams and had the courage to shine bright. And I'm here to reaffirm that we can all do this.

Maybe we won't all start a business and make just under a million in the first year. We're all on our own journey, and it happens for us all in different ways.

It took me over five years to make a million in a year. For the first two years I made hardly any money because I focused on building my platform, getting in front of my audience, and getting women involved in FEA. It was tough financially, but I could see the light at the end of the tunnel, even though sometimes it seemed a little dim!

Also, in my opinion, the value that you're adding to others should be the focus rather than the money. This is because the more you follow your heart and serve your audience the best you possibly can, the more the money follows anyway and the more rewarding it all is, because of the impact you're having.

Regardless of whether you want to make a million or not, there's one thing I know for sure:

**You can turn your ideas into reality and
build a wildly successful business, because if
one person can do it, we can all do it.**

And, in this part of the book, I'm going to show you exactly how to do that.

It all starts with getting really clear on your idea, your audience, and how you're going to serve them. Then getting out there in front of your audience and sharing your message with them – connecting with them, resonating with them, building a relationship with them.

This is exactly what I did to turn my idea into the business of my dreams. It's what Michelle Rohr did to build a successful business on Etsy. My sister, Sam, and Nikki Elledge Brown did the same, and it's what pretty much every other online entrepreneur I know is doing to build their businesses.

SHE TAKES ACTION

Take the business principles I share in this section and keep asking, 'How can I apply this to my business and make it work?'

EVEN THOUGH
IT'S HARD, IT'S SIMPLE

Let's be real, building a business can be hard work.

You're trying to turn an idea that was in your head into reality.

There are a million and one things to do, most of which you haven't got a clue how to do and it feels incredibly overwhelming and confusing and sometimes even hopeless!

But I want to tell you that despite these very real feelings, it is actually simple.

Most people don't realize this. Most people think that it's waaaaaaay more complicated and it stops them from keeping on going.

I shared a little of Ailish Lucas's story earlier in this book and how she started her organic beauty blog, The Glow Getter… and then how she stopped doing it (see pages 29–31).

For Ailish, there was one simple thing she failed to do the first time around… to be consistent and stick at it. She was so caught up in the doubts and constantly wondering if she was doing the right thing, that she stopped taking consistent action to move forward.

That's all it takes – consistent action to move forward.
That's how you create success on purpose.

About a year later, Ailish decided that she wanted to give the blog another shot, so we chatted all about it and I helped her to make a plan of action for moving forward (that's what you need business friends for!). She created a free beauty guide as a way to get subscribers, she started to send out a weekly email with a video to add value, and she began interviewing beauty brands and doing reviews.

In less than a year she had 1,000 email subscribers, won the Beauty Blogger of the Year Award in the UK, had grown her Facebook audience to 5,000 with the help of Facebook Ads, and she had a ridiculously big bag of free products she'd been sent to review.

Sure, she wasn't making money, yet, and was still freaking out inside about how she'd do that, but she was on her way, big time.

When you keep going and you stay consistent, that's when the momentum builds.

Crazy things begin to happen that you could never have foreseen. Yes, you don't know exactly what's going to happen or how things will work out, but the wheels are moving and you're heading in the right direction.

So throughout this entire section and throughout your entire entrepreneurial journey when you get overwhelmed and feel frustrated by it all, take a step back and remember that it's actually simple. You just have to break it all down, take it one step at a time, and keep taking action to move forward.

With all that said, let's get into the five business steps that will help you to become a wildly successful entrepreneur.

STEP ONE:
THE HEART AND SOUL

What's It All About?

A few years ago I was in California with my now husband, Kelin, and we'd gone to Target because he wanted to get some Bar Keepers Friend to remove a stain in the kitchen. It wasn't exactly a shopping trip that excited me, until I spotted a collection of cleaning products by The Honest Company.

My eyes lit up as I excitedly walked over to them; the range of cleaning products were even cuter in real life. Up until that point I'd only ever seen them online, either being advertised, talked about by Jessica Alba, or on social media.

I carefully started to pick up each product, taking everything in, while trying to decide what I was going to buy. Lost in my thoughts, I was interrupted by Kelin asking me what on earth I was doing. I was practically drooling over some cleaning products.

I proceeded to tell him all about The Honest Company and how everything was eco-friendly, safe to use and basically what an amazing company it was. He gave me a confused look and just shrugged his shoulders when I insisted on buying a multi-surface cleaner (that we didn't need and that was way more expensive then the regular surface cleaners).

When we got into the car to drive home, I sat there with my multi-surface cleaner in my hands and Kelin looked over at me and said with a smile on his face, 'You're so proud of yourself, aren't you?'

I smiled back. I was.

So what on earth was going on? Why was I so proud of myself for buying a cleaning product? Why did it make me feel so good and excited – I literally couldn't wait to use it!? Simple! The Honest Company have one heck of an incredible brand, and it's definitely not by accident.

They know what their mission is and what they stand for, they're clear about the value they add and they communicate it so clearly to their audience, in a way that really resonates with them. For this reason, people like me buy it, not because we need it but because we want it, because it resonates with us deeply… and we're talking about a cleaning product here, not some cute shoes or an amazing bag!

If The Honest Company can turn boring old cleaning products into exciting purchases, then every single one of us can do the same for our products and services.

It all starts with getting ridiculously clear on what's at the heart and soul of your business – what your mission is, why you're doing it and what you stand for.

I like to call this your Entrepreneurial North Star, because not only will it help you to stay on the right track throughout your journey, it will also attract your dream audience to you.

So, what's your business mission? Why are you doing it? What do you stand for? Let's talk about it.

Your Mission

Before I actually started building FEA, I had messages bubbling up inside of me that I wanted to share with other female entrepreneurs to inspire and empower them. I knew there was an amazing opportunity for me to create something, because there was hardly any support online at the time that was aimed at women in business. I felt so passionately about it, but it all felt a bit hazy and wishy-washy. I knew that if I wanted to turn my idea into a success I had to get clear on what exactly it was that I wanted to do, so I sat down and decided I was going to get clear on my mission by writing it down.

I began by thinking about the big picture of FEA, what I wanted it to look like when it was successful and I realized that the only way I could create a clear vision for myself was if I knew why I was doing it and what it meant to me.

So I began thinking about my why. Why did I have these messages bubbling up inside me? Why did I have a desire to share them? Why did I want to build a platform for female entrepreneurs?

I began to write it all out...

- I want to create something that will have a positive impact.

- I want to create something I'm completely passionate about.

- I want to create something that I can put my entire heart and soul into.

- I want to create something that will inspire me and light me up.

- I want to create something that will enable me to help other women in business, like me, who know the struggle and feel isolated.

- I want to build a business that will enable me to live my dream life — doing something I'm passionate about, having the freedom to work from wherever I want, having the financial abundance to experience amazing things and give to charity.

The list went on and on and on and based on what I felt in the pit of my stomach, I could start to make out what FEA would look like when it was successful.

I knew I wanted to be able to help as many female entrepreneurs from around the world as I possibly could. I knew I wanted to inspire and empower those women to succeed — I knew it was the personal development and inspiration aspect that lit me up, so I knew I wanted to focus on that more than the how-to side.

Based on this realization, I wrote out one simple statement that summed up my FEA business mission and purpose:

'I'm going to inspire and empower as many women as I possibly can from around the world to turn their ideas into reality and build successful businesses.'

I decided that I wanted to make it the biggest and best platform I possibly could.

Once I pulled my mission together and wrote it down on paper, my ideas became tangible for the first time. With my vision clear in my mind, I knew that all I needed to do was take little steps toward fulfilling it. I didn't know everything (far from it; clarity comes from taking action and walking the path), but I knew what was at the heart and soul of my business and why I was building it and that was enough.

This has kept me on track throughout building FEA. Whenever I have a decision to make, let's say an opportunity comes up to do something new, all I have to do is ask myself, 'Does this align with my mission? Will it inspire and/or empower my audience to build a successful business? Is it in alignment with why I'm building FEA?' If the answer is, 'Yes,' I'll consider doing it. If the answer is, 'No,' then I'll decline.

It's my Entrepreneurial North Star leading me where I need to go.

So what's yours?

SHE TAKES ACTION

YOUR WHY

Start by exploring these questions:

* *Why do you want to build your business for you?*

* *What will it mean?*

Perhaps for you it's about creating more financial abundance in your life. Maybe it's about creating a business that gives you the freedom to do what you want, when you want. Maybe it's because you want to be able to spend more time with your family or just create a better life. Maybe it's about doing something you LOVE with your life. Maybe it's because you want to make a difference in the world. Maybe it's because you have a message or a product that you have to share.

Get clear on your why and write it down, as this will help you to keep going when you get lost in the chaos of business and wonder what on earth you're doing it for.

You started your business for a very good reason, so call upon it whenever you need it to keep you on track.

YOUR BUSINESS MISSION

Get clear on your business mission by exploring these questions:

- *What do you want to do?*

- *What's at the heart and soul of your business?*

- *Who are you trying to serve? (We'll talk about this in more depth next, see page 98.)*

- *How are you going to do it?*

Write out what your business mission is in one simple statement:

'I'm going to...[*fill in your mission*].'

This is the beating heart of your idea. It doesn't just exist in your mind anymore – it exists on paper, it exists beyond you.

Getting clear on your personal and business mission in itself is going to help you stay on track, moving in the direction of success, so write out your mission and stick it somewhere you'll see it every single day. It's your Entrepreneurial North Star so don't lose sight of it.

What Do You Stand for?

Over the course of building FEA, I've been on an exploration to get clearer and clearer about what FEA really stands for, what its beliefs and values are (which are ultimately my beliefs and values). Doing this has not only helped me to build a brand that my audience love, because they resonate and connect with it much more deeply, it has also enabled me to build a movement – a movement of women with the same beliefs and purpose as me.

This has been powerful and it's something we can all do (and should all do) in business. It will enable us to have more of an impact.

Here are the beliefs and values written out on the FEA website:

Belief One: Dream Big

Life is not a dress rehearsal. THIS. IS. IT. So we believe that every single one of us should make the absolute most of it and we're here to help you with that. Through our posts, videos, and social updates we're going to help you to dream big and have the courage to go for it.

Belief Two: Believe

When you believe you can do something, it can make you unstoppable. We're going to be the people day-in, day-out that believe in you. We're going to be here championing you on through this very website and all of our social media platforms, so stay connected with us and we'll help you to succeed.

Belief Three: Support and Friendship

We are here for you, to celebrate your successes and to catch you when you fall. We all need a business bestie to celebrate with when things go well, and to see us through and to encourage us to keep going when things don't go so well! We'll be right here for you to keep you strong.

Belief Four: Inspire

We're going to be here to keep you inspired every single day. We're going to empower you with words that ring so true, it will get that fire going inside of you. The one that makes you feel ready to take on the world. The one that makes you feel like you can do it. Because you can, but sometimes it's easy to forget, so we're going to remind you.

Belief Five: Be Real

There's only one of you in the universe. That's a big deal. You are one of a kind and we think you should own it. Around here you can be yourself. Sometimes people can feel like they're not good enough, so they try to be something they're not, but it doesn't work. We believe in authenticity, honesty and integrity.

These five beliefs are entwined in everything we do and create; they give FEA a purpose, which my audience can get behind, because they will have the same beliefs too. It's also helped me to build a business where my audience knows what they can expect, and this has helped me to set FEA apart from other sites for women in business.

So what does your business stand for? What are the beliefs and values at its core? This is an ongoing exploration, so open yourself up to digging deep with it.

SHE TAKES ACTION

Take some time to explore the beliefs and values of your business and write them out. What does your business stand for?

STEP TWO: YOUR AUDIENCE

Who Are Your Audience?

Once you're clear about what your business mission is and what's at the heart and soul of it, the next thing you need to get really clear about is who your audience are, who you want to serve, who you're trying to get your message and business in front of.

One of the reasons why The Honest Company is so successful is because they're so clear about who their audience are and they do everything with their target audience in mind. Their products are definitely not for everyone and they don't try to be.

Their target audience is someone who believes in using non-toxic products in their home. They are proud of their home and want things to look good – I'm sure there's more to their audience than this, but the point is that they've created their products for that person.

I was compelled to buy one of their products because it resonated with me on every level, because I am their target audience and I have the same beliefs and ideals as them.

I believe that the products I use should be non-toxic and eco-friendly, and so do they.

I strive to make my home feel good and look beautiful. Their products strive to do the same thing. They look stylish, not like 'normal' cleaning products.

These things make me feel like me and this brand belong together.

You want your audience to feel like they belong with you and your business. In order to achieve that, you need to know exactly who they are.

When I was starting FEA I knew my audience were women who were thinking about starting a business or already running a business. But that was about all I knew and there was a massive part of me that thought, 'Maybe I should just create something to inspire everyone! I'd love to help children and teenagers to feel inspired and empowered, and I'd love to help people realize their dreams!' I felt passionate about helping lots of different people and I think this is something a lot of us feel – we want to help and appeal to everyone.

However, this is a recipe for disaster, because the way you communicate with a child is totally different to the way you'd communicate with an adult. And you'd probably communicate differently with a woman than you would with a man. So, if we try to please everyone, we're actually not really resonating much with anyone.

So, while it's good to have dreams about helping everyone, start off by getting laser focused on one particular audience.

My decision to focus on female entrepreneurs crystalized because everything I seemed to be creating felt completely geared to women. I was using pinks, and I was writing like I was talking with my girlfriends. Sometimes you have to get started taking action to realize what feels like the right thing to do. And just because you're narrowing your focus now, doesn't mean you can't widen it later on, so don't worry about that.

When I started to think more about who my audience was, I realized I didn't know her challenges, her dreams, desires, or fears. So, initially, I took some time to think about who she might be. Since I had no one to ask, because I hadn't actually put FEA out there, I set aside some time to write about her and get to know her. I started by thinking about the following things in relation to her starting and building a business:

- What are her desires? What does she want to achieve?

- What's holding her back?

- What are her challenges – internal (i.e. specific doubts and worries she has, like not feeling good enough, not believing she can make it happen) and external (i.e. things going on around her that might be holding her back, maybe she doesn't think she has enough time, or maybe she has a challenge with money, etc.)?

- What are her fears?

- What does she need help with in order to achieve her vision?

I knew that a woman in my audience would have a burning desire to turn her ideas into reality and build a successful business. I knew that she'd probably be feeling quite alone on her journey and would be looking for like-minded people for help and support. I knew that if she were searching on Google for help with building her business, it meant that she wanted someone to show her how to breakthrough, how to up-level, how to actually do it.

I knew all this because that was my personal experience. I knew my own dreams, desires, challenges, and fears, so that was my starting point.

There are so many questions you can ask yourself as you're digging into who your dream audience are.

My friend Nikki asked herself, 'Who would pay me for help with communication?'

That was enough for Nikki to get going, and throughout her journey she's got to know her audience more deeply, as she continues her mission to help entrepreneurs attract their dream clients one brilliant message at a time.

My sister, Sam, ended up realizing the importance of this question once she'd got her business up and running. She started her graphic design business thinking her audience was female entrepreneurs, only to realize a year later that the entrepreneurs she seemed to be attracting had no money to pay her.

So she decided to go back to the drawing board and rethink who she wanted her audience to be. Since starting her business, she'd got married and designed her own wedding stationery, which sparked the idea of using her graphic design skills to design wedding invites – something that brides were definitely prepared to pay for.

You don't have to have it all perfectly figured out, and sometimes people get started thinking their audience is one person, only to discover later on that it's someone else. This is exactly what happened to Michelle Rohr.

In the early days of running her blog, Michelle thought her audience was college dropouts. People, like her, who went to college and decided it wasn't for them, quit, but then had no clue what to do next. So everything she was creating was aimed at those people. Then after a year or so, Michelle decided to survey her audience and find out more about who was reading her blog. She was shocked when she discovered it wasn't college dropouts, it was women in their 30s and 40s, who had a desire to take 100 percent responsibility for their lives. Once she found this out, she adjusted the content she was delivering, so it would resonate more with her actual audience.

Remember, you can adjust as you build. It's all an evolution.

It's all a journey, with twists and turns, so do what you can now with what you know, to get as clear as possible about who your audience are and dig deeper as you go.

The main reason why you want to understand your audience as much as possible is because throughout your entrepreneurial journey you'll need to take your lead from them.

So many entrepreneurs get this part wrong, they think their business is all about them – their dreams, their desires, their goals – but if you want to make your business a success then you have to shift your focus from yourself to your audience.

Your business is not about you; it's about them – your wonderful audience. It's about their needs, their desires, their problems and challenges, and it's up to you to understand them as much as possible.

**The more connected you are with your audience,
the more you'll be able to resonate with them.**

Once you begin to build your audience, through social media, email subscribers, customers etc., you can begin to survey them to find out more about their dreams, desires, challenges, and fears. I love asking my fans, followers, and subscribers, 'what's your number one frustration as an entrepreneur right now? Where are you at in your business journey? What would you love help with right now?'

I constantly ask my audience questions, via my Facebook page and through surveys, so that I can understand where they're at in more detail.

The answers I receive are like gold dust, because they tell me in their exact words what I can do to help them more. In the past, I've used the words that people have written in survey responses in my website copy and posts, because it communicates exactly how so many of the women in my audience actually feel, and then I get messages back from them saying, 'It's like you read my mind.'

Keep this simple and just do all you can throughout your journey to get to know your audience the best you can.

SHE TAKES ACTION

Take some time now to think about who your audience are, who will resonate with your business and ultimately want to become a fan, follower, subscriber, and customer. Here are some questions to help you to explore:

- *Who are your audience?*

- *Where do they live?*

- *What's their gender?*

- *What do they do?*

- *What kind of people are they?*

- *What's going on in their lives?*

- *What age are they?*

- *Why would they want what you have to offer?*

- *What are their desires?*

- *What are their pain points/challenges/frustrations (internal and external)?*

- *Why will your business help them/appeal to them?*

Once you're clearer about who your audience are, simplify it all by creating your dream audience profile, for example:

- *She's in her twenties or thirties.*

- *She wants to feel more inspired.*

- *She has a burning desire to live an incredible life.*

- *She wants help to move past the challenges holding her back – fear, lack of time, money, competency, etc.*

- *She wants to turn her ideas into reality.*

- *She wants to build a really successful business.*

- *She wants to connect with people who share her vision.*

- *She wants to learn and grow as a person.*

- *She wants to know that she's not alone – that there are other people out there just like her, who can help take her to another level.*

- *She's looking for help and support to be more successful.*

Remember, you don't need to know everything, just get started with it and learn more as you go.

You Can't Please Everyone

*'You can be the ripest, juiciest peach in the world, but
there will always be someone who hates peaches.'*

DITA VON TEESE

I remember when I was sitting in the coffee shop, ready to launch my magazine to the world, and a guy who was working there introduced me to a woman who was just about to launch her own business.

She'd quit the finance world to start up her own venture. I excitedly showed her the magazine I was literally just about to launch. I began flicking through the pages showing her everything and telling her about it. She was the first stranger that had seen it, so I was excited to hear what she thought.

The first thing she said was, 'Wow,' and I thought, 'Ooooh she loves it, it is pretty wow!'

Then, she followed up with, 'This is soooo patronizing! I really hate pink, it just won't be taken seriously.'

It was like I'd been punched in the stomach. I was literally about to email it out to my subscribers, and here was someone telling me that basically I'd created something that was demeaning women.

Great.

She walked away from the table, and I looked through the magazine again. I thought, 'I've worked so hard to create this, I love pink, and I'm going to post it out.' And so I did. Within minutes, I'd received so many emails from people who'd had a glance and loved it.

The response was incredible, and that magazine became so loved by so many people.

BUT, some people hated it.

You can't please everyone, and you shouldn't even try to.

I created that magazine from my heart. I love pink, and I don't find it demeaning in any way whatsoever – it's just a color – and I wanted to be able to create something where I could express myself authentically. And, in doing so, I attracted more of my tribe to me, the people who I really wanted to have on board.

Know that you won't please everyone, which is why it's incredibly helpful to get clear on who you are actually trying to please, who you think would LOVE your message. These are the people you want on board.

STEP THREE:
ENGAGING YOUR AUDIENCE

How to Make Your Audience Fall in Love

Once you know who your audience are, the next thing you need to do is communicate your business mission and purpose with them in a way that will connect and resonate with them so much, it makes them fall in love with your business.

How do you do this? Through what you create and put out there to them. From the look and feel of everything (your website, your social media posts, your products/services/freebies), to how your serve your audience (the content, products and services you put out there), to the experience you craft for them.

Everything you create needs to align with your core message (your mission + purpose) and resonate with your audience. It needs to add value, it needs to wow and delight them.

The more you do this and the better you become at it, the more your audience will love your business and want to become fans, followers, subscribers and customers.

Think about the brands you love right now and ask yourself why you love them. When you first discovered them, what did they do that intrigued you and made you want to find out more? What made you begin to like what you saw? If you became a fan, subscriber or customer, ask yourself why. What did they do that compelled you so much?

Maybe it was that you loved their site and what an amazing or easy experience they'd created for you. Maybe it was that their message hit you hard and made you think, 'Yes, I totally get that.'

No matter what it was, there's one thing I know for sure – they didn't get you to fall in love with their brand by accident. They made it happen on purpose, and this is what you have to do with your business too.

So, let's get started.

Delight Your Audience

'Pretend that every single person you meet has a sign around his or her neck that says, 'Make me feel important.' Not only will you succeed in sales, you will succeed in life.'
MARY KAY ASH

When I was starting FEA, I knew what I wanted to do, I knew who my target audience were, but I had no idea how I was going to start connecting and resonating with them. I didn't know how to begin building a relationship with them, so they were aware of what my business stood for and so could decide whether it was something they wanted to be part of.

What I did know was that I needed to figure this out!

I knew that somehow I had to find a way to resonate and connect with my audience so deeply that they were delighted with FEA. I had to go above and beyond to make them fall in love with my business by creating a wonderful experience for them and by serving them to the best of my ability.

We all have to do this. The more you can connect and resonate with your audience in a way that delights them, the more successful you will become, because you'll have an impact on those people – they'll want to get to know you/your business more. Maybe they'll tell their friends and family about your company, maybe they'll love what you're doing so much they'll want to become subscribers, fans, followers, and customers.

A couple of years ago while walking around London, I stumbled across a shop called Jo Loves, which was the latest venture of Jo Malone. As I walked through the door, delicious, sweet smells floated up around me. (You wouldn't expect anything less from a perfumer.) The glass shelves around the edge of the room exquisitely displayed the perfumes, body washes, and candles that were for sale. The packaging was beautiful, and the staff were warm and inviting. I fell in love with the Jo Loves store.

In the middle of the store was what they called the Jo Loves Fragrance Brasserie Bar, which in their words was, 'Designed to amuse your nose and scent your skin.' They called it Fragrance Tapas.

They weren't just selling perfumes and candles. The moment you walked through the door, they were sharing an experience with you. You could tell that so much love had gone into everything they'd created for you, the customer.

After trying out the Fragrance Tapas and hearing the stories behind the scents, I was completely sold. I bought my mum some body wash for her birthday and watched as they carefully packaged it into a box, put the box in a beautiful bag, and then placed tissue paper inside, which they sprayed with one of their perfumes.

For the rest of the day, I walked around London with the experience of Jo Loves very much following me around. When I got home, I told my family about the store and how incredible it was.

That's the power of branding, and that's exactly what we all need to strive for as entrepreneurs.

When you set out to turn your idea into reality, you're not just creating a business; you're creating your brand, and your brand is all about how you make your audience and customers feel – what they think of when they think about your business, when they interact with your business, when they talk about your business.

Your idea/message/business/product isn't just a thing; it's an experience someone has with you and it's your job to go above and beyond to make that experience delightful for your audience.

Whether you have a product, a service, a physical store, or just an online presence, every word you write, every little thing you create, must make your audience fall more in love with you, because you delight them.

From how everything looks, to the words you use, to the personal touches you create.

My sister, Sam, goes above and beyond to make the customer experience phenomenal for brides-to-be. From the beautiful website and graphics she's created, to the sweet, warm and friendly emails she sends her prospective customers and existing customers, to the way she packages up the samples and invites she sends out.

The attention to detail with what she does is on another level. From the way the invites are laid out, to the box they sit in, to the custom-printed Little Green paper it's all wrapped in – it looks like an exciting parcel and brides fill with excitement when it arrives at their door, because Sam has put so much love and care into it all. Sam knows this, because her customers have emailed her to tell her.

Over the years of building FEA, I've loved figuring out what I can do to make my audience resonate, connect and fall more in love with what I'm creating.

From the inspirational graphics we post out on Facebook and the content that's published on the website, to the way the website looks and feels, to the way I create my emails… I'm always thinking about the experience I'm creating for my audience. I'm always asking myself, 'Will this inspire and empower my audience to build an amazing business? Will this add value? Will this resonate with them? Will this create more trust?'

I'm constantly thinking about ways I can love my audience more. They mean everything to me and I want to make sure that they know it.

This doesn't have to be complicated, just think about the small things you can do that will delight your audience.

For me (and every other entrepreneur out there) figuring out how to delight my audience has been an ongoing evolution. It's a never-ending journey, so all we can do is keep pressing into the question, 'What can I do to express the values, meaning and feeling of my brand to my audience in a way that will resonate with them and build more likability and trust?'

SHE TAKES ACTION

So how do you want your audience to feel when they come into contact with your business? What experience do you want to create for them? What do you want your brand to mean to your audience? How will you show your love and care for your audience?

Write it down and get clear about it, so that you can weave these things into everything you create for your business from this point forward.

Expressing Your Brand

'People spend money when and where they feel good.'
WALT DISNEY

Once you've got a clear idea of what your brand stands for and how you want to make your audience feel, you have to figure out how you're going to express it, how you're going to engage your audience with it.

How are you going to express it through your website, through your marketing, through your messaging, through your product or service delivery?

How are you going to communicate your brand clearly through every little thing you do?

At the beginning, I had no idea. So I dug around online, looking at websites of brands I loved, brands I subscribed to, brands I bought from, I looked at their social media accounts too and I paid attention to how they were communicating their brand so well, that it made me LOVE them.

As I described in the previous chapter (see page 90), I realized that it had a lot to do with presentation.

The brands I loved the most were consistent in their messaging, in the colors, fonts and images they used — all of these things were helping me to have a deeper and more meaningful connection with them. All of these things were doing a good job at expressing their brand.

So I got to work on figuring out how I could do a good job at expressing my brand.

I knew I wanted everything I created to be beautiful and feminine and to feel positive and inspiring. At the beginning, I didn't really know how to do this, but over the years I began to create mood boards where I got clear on the colors, the fonts, the patterns, and the styles I wanted to use. I started a Pinterest board where I pinned images of how I thought FEA should feel. I cultivated a clear visual feeling for FEA. I used pink, coral, and gold. I used beautiful fonts, patterns, and images. I wanted to make sure that whenever we created and posted out an image for FEA, people would know it was FEA, because it had a distinct and consistent feel.

While the feel and style of FEA has evolved — as everything does — we've been consistent in the goal of creating beautiful, feminine, and empowering content and graphics across every platform where we're visible (our website, emails, social media, packaging etc.). People now say, 'That's very FEA' — but it took a good four years before I ever heard someone say it.

SHE TAKES ACTION

So how are you going to express your brand to ensure your audience resonate with it?

- *What's your style?*

- *What colors will you use?*

- *What fonts will you use?*

Create a mood board, or start one on Pinterest, and pin images that represent your brand – whether it's a color palette, a font, a bunch of flowers that feels like your brand… whatever it is.

Get creative and work on expressing your brand in the best way you possibly can.

Communicating with Your Audience

As well as being able to express your brand effectively and look good, you also have to figure out how to invite your audience to want to get to know you more, whether that's becoming a fan, follower, subscriber, repeat visitor or customer.

You don't want people within your target audience to discover you, only to forget about you, because you didn't proactively encourage the relationship to develop.

Put simply, how are you going to compel the people who come across you to stick around and get to know you more?

The answer is simple. By communicating your message with them, serving them to the best of your ability and giving them a call to action (asking them to stick around in some form).

If you don't ask, you don't get, and in this noisy online world, where our brands largely exist, we have to do all we can to get our audience to want more from us.

For every page of your website you create, every blog post you write, every video you make, every social media post you publish, every email you send out, basically every message, product and service (free and paid) you put out there to your audience, you need to know:

- Exactly what you want people to know

- How you want to make them feel

- What value you'll add or what transformation you'll give them

- What action you want them to take

For example, on my website, I have a home page, where my goal is to let my visitor know what FEA is about, to make her feel like she's landed in the right place and found something that she resonates with (primarily through the way it looks and feels and through the words I use), and to show her the latest value proposition we have, such as the blog posts, videos, free downloads etc. I give her a call to action to get her to click into a post, and I also have a 'Getting Started' image right at the top, if she's never visited the site before, so I can explain to her what FEA is and how it can help her.

I have an 'About' page, where my goal is to let her know how FEA can help her and the story behind the community. I want to make her feel like the community is perfect for her by connecting with her desires and challenges and giving her the call to action to get involved, by becoming a free subscriber.

The 'About' page is one of the most important on your website, because if people discover you and are intrigued, then they'll want to find out more about who you are.

On my website, I have installed a free app called SumoMe, which enables me to use Heat Maps on my site, this allows me to see where people are clicking. I noticed that on the home page, people were getting to the bottom and then clicking on the 'About' link, wanting to find out more. So, I tweaked the footer on the website to include a little bit of information about FEA, an image of me, and a link to click to find out more about getting started with FEA, plus a link to learn more about FEA and myself. If you don't use Heat Maps, definitely try it out.

The biggest lesson I've learned is that you're doing your visitor such a huge disservice if you fail to communicate clearly the wonderful things that you can offer her, both free and paid (plus, you've worked so hard to create them!). If you don't spell it out, she won't know it's there. You have to make it as easy as possible for her to want to hang around and get to know you more – on every page of your site.

I also use the SumoMe app to enable pop-ups on my website, so if someone visits my site for the first time, she'll see a pop-up at some point, which will ask her if she wants to sign up for 'a weekly dose of inspiration to help build a successful business.' Too many people are worried about annoying their audience by adding pop-ups, but again, if you don't ask, the answer is always NO. My pop-up has generated over 25,000 email subscribers for FEA – as of right now, pop-ups work.

You need to be leveraging your website effectively, as a way to communicate with your audience and get them to want to hang out with you more (whether it's that you compel them to come back and visit again, whether it's that you get them to become a subscriber, whether it's that you get them to buy) and you can do that by ensuring that you're clear about a few key things.

- What do you want your visitors to know?

- How do you want them to feel?

- How will you add value?

- What do you want them to do while they're there?

This is something I learned from my copy expert friend Nikki. She also says to ask your friends or your audience to take a look at specific pages of your website and ask them:

- What did you take away?

- How did the page make you feel?

- What action did you feel compelled to take, if any?

Just keep tweaking as you go – I am always tweaking and testing new ways to communicate my message better to my audience.

Not only do you need to communicate effectively on your website, you need to communicate effectively through all other channels too, such as social media, Facebook Ads, videos, workshops, guides and worksheets – whatever is relevant to you.

On my social media, I have a variety of different posts going out to communicate the message and purpose of FEA:

- Inspirational quotes, messages and questions to inspire and empower – the aim of these is to get people to like and share them. I do this by sharing the best quotes and creating the best graphics. Sometimes I'll write, 'Tag a friend who needs this message today' or 'How true is this? Hit like if you think so!'

- Blog posts – when I share these via social media, I create beautiful graphics to go along with them and I have to make sure the text I'm sharing is compelling and gives the follower a call to action to read more on the website.

- Promotions – when I'm sharing an offer (free or paid) on social media, like an upcoming free workshop I'm hosting or enrollment to the Members' Club, I create beautiful graphics and really think about the message I'm sharing – will it resonate? Does it state clearly what action I want people to take? Is it in alignment with my brand? How will it make my audience feel? Inspired, excited, fired up?

Ultimately, no matter what I'm creating and sharing with my audience, I always try and get clear about how it will make them feel, how it will add value and what action it will encourage them to take.

If you make it your priority to ensure what you create and share is doing a spectacular job at communicating your message, then your tribe of fans, subscribers and customers will grow.

SHE TAKES ACTION

Take time to go over your website and ask yourself if it's doing a good job at communicating your message and resonating with your audience. Get feedback from your friends and audience and keep working on making it better.

This book isn't about teaching you how to create an amazing website, but if you need help with this then we have free master classes you can watch on FEA here http://bit.ly/SMB-Resources to help you get everything set up.

Next go over your social media profiles and ask yourself:

- *When someone comes to my profile how do I want to make them feel?*

- *Am I achieving this?*

- *What action do I want them to take? How am I going to get them to take it?*

Serving Your Audience

You heard Kimra's story in an earlier chapter (see page 81), and how, within the space of a year, she'd built an audience of thousands of fans and hundreds of customers, but how?

The answer: She built authority, credibility, and a deep relationship with her audience by serving them with free content and paid products and services, consistently. What she created for them impressed them, and people began to know her, love her, and trust her. People began to talk about her and tell their friends about her. People wanted to interview her and share her story and tips. People wanted to connect with her.

The thing is, people take away what you put out, so if you want to succeed you need to be putting good stuff out there!

Here's what Kimra was putting out there to her audience to serve and add value:

- She created a free webinar to teach people how to create graphics using PicMonkey. She had nothing to sell, but she did have some good advice to give, and she went for it.

- She prepared the content she was going to share during the webinar and set up a registration page, so people could sign up and join her for it.

- She shared the page in Facebook groups and using Facebook Ads and people began to sign up. She had 200 sign-ups, 100 of those people joined her live, and they loved it. They left comments saying how amazing the webinar was and how much value they got from it.

A week later Kimra decided to host another, and then another, and then another. For a whole year, Kimra did a webinar every week (give or take a couple).

She paid attention to her audience to see what they were struggling with, and she created free webinars to help them – webinars that resonated with them so much, it was like she'd read their minds. The more action she took to serve her audience, the more she started to realize how much she had to give, the more her audience fell in love with her and became raving fans.

When you have an idea, a message, and business you want to share, you have to communicate it with your audience. Your aim is to intrigue, compel, and delight them, so that they want to find out more about you and what you have to offer. You have to get them to buy into what you're creating. When you do this well, these people will become your tribe of raving fans and customers.

The more people you can get to join your tribe, the more impact you can have, and the more success you can create.

Thankfully, in this digital age, doing what Kimra did – going from unknown to having a tribe of raving fans – is doable for all of us.

When I started FEA, no one knew me or what my message was, so I leveraged the Internet like crazy in order to build up my tribe. Within a few years, I've gone from having an idea that only existed in my head, to having a network of over 300,000 female entrepreneurs who resonate with the mission of FEA. They've come to love what I've created.

There's one main thing I've done in order to make this happen. I've exchanged the most valuable currency there is – value itself. I've gone above and beyond to serve my audience.

I now have a three-step process for how I do this:

1. **Free content** – e.g. blog posts, weekly videos on YouTube, inspirational graphics, and tips on social media. These are available to everyone online.

2. **Free goods** – e.g. fun worksheets, printables, wallpapers, workshops, visualizations. These are available to my subscribers. So people sign up via email to receive the goods, which enables me to build my email subscribers, which in turn allows me to communicate more effectively with my audience, so I can build a better relationship with them.

3. **Paid goods** – e.g. my Members' Club (which offers monthly trainings and an online community) and physical products, such as my inspirational wall prints and my annual wall planner.

All of the above enable me to serve and add value to my audience at the same time as communicating the message of FEA with them. Typically the journey for someone who doesn't know of FEA, to them becoming a fan and customer, will go like this…

Someone will stumble across my Facebook fan page, website, or YouTube channel, and she'll quickly get a feel for FEA, and realize that she'll find inspiration and support along her entrepreneurial journey.

She resonates and connects with my free content and is intrigued enough to want to see what else we have going on. She might become a fan of my Facebook page, and/or she'll head over to the website.

Whether she's on my Facebook page or my website, I share more value and communicate the free content and goods we have that she might love. I give her a call to action, asking her to subscribe to FEA's email list.

From there, I continue to build the relationship with her, by emailing her once a week and sharing a video post with tips to help her build her business (adding value) and through emails communicating what else we have that she might love, such as the Members' Club. As the weeks go by, she comes to know me and FEA more, and the connection becomes stronger. (Or she'll decide that I'm not her cup of tea, and we'll part ways, which is completely OK.)

At some point, she may decide that she wants to get more involved and join the Members' Club, which means she'll be a paying customer – an integral part of any business model.

Sometimes, the journey to get her to join the FEA tribe takes a long time. Some people see my content and it might take them several times of stumbling over it before they take notice and decided to come in further. Other times, people might see a Facebook Ad I've created that communicates the value and message of FEA and they fall in love right away and can't wait to be part of it.

No matter how long it takes, it's still a journey I have to take people on. I use words, images, videos, my website and social media profiles to communicate effectively what's at the heart and soul of FEA. I have to do such a good job, so that what I create delights them, adds value for them, and compels them to want to come in a little further.

In one way or another, we all have to do this. In the online business world, especially for service-based businesses, creating free content like blog posts, videos, podcasts and printables (checklists, worksheets, guides, eBooks etc.) is a brilliant way to begin delivering value to your audience.

The better we get at doing this, the more credibility and authority we'll build and the more raving fans and customers we'll have.

So let's talk more about this.

My First Creation

When I started FEA, I had no real clue how to get my audience to buy into my vision, my message, and my business. But one of the reasons for starting FEA was, as I've described, because I felt so lonely building an online business, so I decided to go on the hunt for female entrepreneurs with an inspiring story to share, and that's how I first started to add value and serve my audience.

As it happened, the first story I ever published was about a girl who had such a similar journey to me. Like me, she'd studied Law, set up an online technology business, and was in her twenties.

For the first time, I realized that I wasn't alone. There was someone else out there who was just like me, and it inspired me so much. It gave me a confidence that, somehow, I was totally on the right track.

Since then, I've gone on to add value to my audience in so many ways.

At the beginning of 2012, I'd been publishing stories for about a year and it was going amazingly well. Still, I felt my niggle whispering, 'step up' in my ear. Then my sister forwarded me a link to an online magazine and my brain went into overdrive, as I began to get excited about the idea of creating my own online magazine for female entrepreneurs. I knew it could add huge value and take FEA to another level – I could feel it. I wanted to make it free, as well, so that I could use it to reach as many women as possible and use it as a way to build up my email list and my community, and get people talking about FEA and what we were creating.

I had zero idea how to create or publish an online magazine, but I was 100 percent committed to doing it. As I've mentioned already, when you commit, the universe has a way of showing up to help. Within days of deciding to create the magazine, a girl called Natalie Walstein submitted her story to be featured on the website. She also happened to be a graphic designer and had worked on designing digital magazines. I thought, 'Thank you, universe, I've just found my designer!'

I had absolutely no idea what to call the magazine but thankfully, my sister, Sam, came to the rescue and suggested *This Girl Means Business*, a blog she'd started to run on my website a few months earlier.

I loved it.

My FEA mission was clearer than ever before, after spending a year working on it, and I mapped out exactly how I wanted the magazine to inspire and empower women. I thought about how I wanted it to leave people feeling, and based on that, I got an idea as to what kind of articles and features needed to go in the magazine, what kind of tone they needed to have, and what kind of colors and design elements we needed to use to make sure the magazine had the impact that I wanted it to have. I wanted it to be beautiful.

Next, I started to work on my wish list of amazing people I wanted to feature on the front cover, as I described earlier (see page 71).

I also reached out to other inspiring entrepreneurs I'd connected with over the previous year and featured more stories, I wrote some articles, we added some inspirational quotes, and we ended on a feature called '10 Things to Remember on Your Journey.' Within a few short months, Issue 1 of *This Girl Means Business* was finished.

When Natalie sent over the final designs, it was perfect, exactly what I had envisioned. There I was, sitting in a coffee shop in London on Friday, June 29 2012, about to launch my idea to the world and do something massive to add value to my audience. I was terrified, but I was also really excited.

At 5.28 p.m., I hit 'send,' and my idea was out there.

The power of being seen and heard

After I'd been producing my magazine for a while I decided I wanted to do more to get my message out there in front of my audience and really connect and serve them. So I took a step back to see what was really working well for other people, and also paid attention to the advice people were giving me about how they were creating their tribes of raving fans. Time and time again it was the people who were getting themselves out there via video that were having the biggest impact and seeing the biggest results. I knew then that I too needed to start making videos, sharing valuable tips to inspire and empower my audience to build successful businesses.

My first video was horrific. I looked so stiff and I sounded bored. I knew I could never share it. So I made another one and another, until eventually I decided to share one with my audience. I learned how to edit in iMovie and then uploaded it to YouTube, I created a blog post on my website and embedded the video. Then, I wrote an email to my subscribers. It took me about 30 minutes to actually hit the send button because I was so nervous! But I sent out the email, and the response was amazing, I received the sweetest emails.

Since then I've persevered with it and more or less made a video a week, and while I don't get masses of views, it has helped me to create so much authority and credibility. The women in my audience feel like they know me, because they do!

This came home to me at an event, when a girl came up to me when I was washing my hands in the bathroom and said, 'Are you Carrie Green?' And when I nodded, she proceeded to tell me that she was a massive fan and loved my videos and asked if she could get a picture with me.

It was the most surreal moment ever, but that's the power of video. When you let people in, the relationship becomes so much more valuable. I know that so many people watch my videos for months and months and then eventually decide to join the Members' Club, because the videos establish authority, credibility and trust. Maybe you're reading this book right now, because you've been watching my videos :-)

I realize that creating videos isn't for everyone, but let's just take a look at the stats. In 2014, video accounted for 64 percent of the world's Internet traffic and by 2019 Cisco predicts that figure will be 80 percent.

That's why more people are sharing their message via video – sharing tutorials, tips, messages, experiences, and behind the scenes. There's so much you can do with video. Yes, it feels awkward at first, but the impact video can have is phenomenal.

Ailish began creating organic beauty video tutorials in 2015. After the fourth video she published to YouTube, she received an email from a large online retailer in the organic beauty world, saying they loved her videos and asked if she would be interested in talking to them about her making videos for them!

Kimra engaged the power of video, but in a slightly different way; she used live Google hangouts instead of pre-recorded videos. Every week, when she hosted her webinars, people got to see and hear her. They started to feel like they knew her. Obviously, if she'd shared dreadful advice and tips, people would have switched off, but as she was sharing great content it helped to cement her authority and credibility, week in and week out.

Some people prefer creating podcasts, instead of creating videos, and those are incredibly valuable, too, because the number of people who listen to podcasts is going up and up and up.

In 2012 John Lee Dumas set about creating a daily podcast show, where he would share an inspiring interview with an entrepreneur. It came about because he went looking for a daily podcast sharing an interview with an entrepreneur and couldn't find one, so he decided to create one himself.

He crafted out the concept for his show, he wrote out who his perfect listener was and he decided to create free, valuable content, consistently. The Entrepreneur on Fire Podcast was born and soon after that his tribe, that he now calls his Fire Nation, began to develop. His listeners loved his daily podcasts and subscribed to his show. They began to get to know, like and trust him more and since then he's grown from just having a podcast, to having various online products, such as his flagship product Podcasters' Paradise, where he teaches people how to start their own successful podcast.

Since starting his podcast in 2012, John now has a huge tribe of fans and a business that generates seven figures a year. This is the power of being heard and getting your message out in front of an audience who want to listen.

You could also do this through speaking on stage, but it's likely that the number of people you can reach through speaking gigs is significantly smaller than the number of people you can reach online.

I'm not saying everyone needs to make videos, podcasts, or speak – I know plenty of successful business people who have never made a public appearance – but video and podcasts are two huge resources and will work no matter what your business is.

Ultimately, there are lots of ways for us all to add value and engage with our audience, it's just about deciding what you're going to create and then creating it.

So let's talk more about it.

How Will You Add Value?

Since starting FEA in 2011, I've dared to push myself outside of my comfort zone, more and more, to find ways to add value to my audience and grow my business. I create weekly videos, I share inspiring quote graphics on Facebook, I create free challenges, checklists, blog posts, workshops, I've also created the Members' Club (our paid service), and now I'm writing this book. All of these things are about communicating my message to my audience and adding value.

Ailish started off by thinking about what one thing she could create, one time, that her audience would love, something that would solve their problems. So she created a free beauty guide and focused on getting it out there. Once she'd created that, she focused on continuing to add value, frequently, by creating weekly video tutorials.

Kimra focused on adding value through hosting a free weekly online workshop, where she taught live the lessons she'd learned and addressed the biggest struggles she knew her audience faced.

Michelle focused on adding value through creating free monthly printables to help her audience take 100 percent responsibility for their life. Literally just a one-page worksheet that would get them to ask themselves questions to help them move forward.

When Nikki got started, she focused on adding value through sharing great tips and advice and by building genuine friendships in Facebook groups.

There are so many different ways for us all to add value to our audience and how we go about it will be different for all of us, depending on the type of business we run.

But bear these three steps in mind:

1. What free content are you spreading around the Internet, as a way to get people to discover you? This could be blog posts that will help people to find you in the Google search, videos that people come across on YouTube or Facebook, posts you share via social media, etc.

2. What free goods are you creating that people have to sign up for to access? Such as a checklist of your top tips, or an eBook, guide or worksheet, or a free video series sharing how-to tips, a webinar, a special offer.

3. What paid products/services are you creating for your audience?

With my sister's wedding stationery business, here's what she does:

1. **Free content:** She shares beautiful graphics on Instagram, which communicate and express her business. She also creates free videos, giving tips for brides-to-be – these videos enable her audience to see her and hear her, which helps to develop the relationship and trust people have for her.

2. **Free goods:** She also has a series of free checklists for brides-to-be, helping them prepare for their big day. Once they subscribe via email she's then able to communicate with them via email, enabling her to build the relationship with them and share what she's created with them.

3. **Paid goods:** She then creates her wedding stationery range with her dream audience in mind. People can buy samples first, to get a taste of how amazing the invites are before purchasing.

With everything she creates, she's constantly crafting an incredible experience, adding value and communicating her message so well, in order to compel her audience to want to buy from her.

It's all about adding value consistently.

At the beginning, when you're creating content and putting it out there, and hardly anyone is seeing it, reading it or engaging with it, it's easy to feel disheartened and like it's all pointless. But you have to keep going, keep being consistent, and keep creating goodness to put out there. As you do, momentum will build. Just stick with it.

SHE TAKES ACTION

So what will you create?

- *How are you getting your message out there and serving your audience?*

- *What could you create that would solve your audience's struggles?*

- *What could you create that would delight them?*

There are so many options to choose from, so go through the following list and note down what you're interested in doing and then pick your top one or two and give yourself permission to focus exclusively on becoming amazing at doing them.

CREATING FREE CONTENT

- *Writing blog posts*

- *Creating videos*

- *Doing a podcast*

- *Hosting live workshops/webinars/streaming*

- *Graphics/posts for social media*

CREATING FREE GOODS TO SIGN UP FOR

- *Printables, such as guides, workbooks, checklists*

- *An eBook*

- *A video training series*

- *An online summit*

- *A webinar*
- *An audio program*
- *A free taster course*
- *A free sample*

Your paid products and services also serve your audience too, don't forget that.

Just remember to go above and beyond to create content that your audience will LOVE. Serve them like never before.

Be YOU

'Be yourself no matter what. Some will adore you and some will hate everything about you. But who cares? It's your life. Make the most out of it.'
UNKNOWN

Over the years of creating value for my audience, I've found it so easy to take a look around at what other people are doing and think, 'I should be more like that person.'

I remember once watching someone else's videos on YouTube and thinking how fun, loud, and entertaining she was. She was sharing great business knowledge, but in such a fun way, and her audience loved her.

Afterwards, I had this feeling of panic, because my videos are nothing like that. It's literally just me talking to the camera. I'm not funny, I'm not loud, and I'm not particularly entertaining, but I felt I should be more of those things having watched her videos.

But, then, I realized *that's not me*. I will never be very funny, I will never be very loud, and I'll probably never be that entertaining. After thinking about it, I realized that I'm OK with that. I realized that I just need to be good at doing *me* well.

I took some time to figure out what made me, me by asking, what are my strengths?

- I'm quiet and mostly softly spoken, and some people really like that, because they can relate.

- I'm completely honest about the experiences I have, and I don't ever sugarcoat things.

- I try to simplify everything I teach. I may not be funny, but at least I can be helpful!

- I don't see myself as the expert who's dictating what to do. I'm the best friend who's right by your side, experimenting with you and sharing what I've learned.

All these things were my strengths and made me, me.

There are so many other women building platforms, blogs, and communities for female entrepreneurs. Essentially, they're my competition, but I don't see it that way because we're all doing it differently. Some people are drawn to FEA because of the way I do things, the energy behind it all, and because they resonate with me. Other people are more attracted to other sites for women in business because they resonate more with the other person. That's totally fine.

So, just focus on being your wonderful, marvelous, amazing, authentic self. The more authentic you are, the more you'll attract the right people to your tribe. If you're anything but, people will see right through you!

SHE TAKES ACTION

Write down what makes you, you. Who is your authentic self?

- *What makes you amazing and special?*

- *What are your strengths?*

Focus on being more you and the world will love you even more. Play to your strengths.

STEP FOUR:
BUILDING YOUR AUDIENCE

The Internet Is Your Stage, Get Out There and Shine

'If you build it, he will come' is the ethereal message that inspires Iowa farmer Ray Kinsella to mow down his cornfield and build a baseball pitch in the movie, *Field of Dreams*.

However, in business, it definitely doesn't work this way. Building a beautiful website, even creating an incredible offering for your audience, isn't enough. Once you've created it, you have to play big and do all you can to get it out there.

Build it, yes, and then get it out there. Then, they will come.

You have to be prepared to promote your business like crazy, in the right way. You have to let people know what you're doing.

When Kimra started to create her weekly webinars, she focused most of her energy on getting in front of her audience and inviting them to join her. She still does the exact same thing now.

When I create new videos, host a workshop, create a worksheet, or create anything, I focus on getting it out there in front of my audience.

There was some research carried out by State of the Business Owner, and they discovered that businesses that focus at least two days a week on marketing their business grow 60 percent faster – which makes complete sense.

Yet, so many people forget to market! They create wonderful things and then play small when it comes to sharing it with their audience. Literally, I've seen people create incredible stuff, but if you went on their website or social media profiles, you'd have no idea that it existed.

First, don't create brilliant things and then not share them – that's just selfish!

Second, once you decide to play big and let your audience know you exist, don't send them on a scavenger hunt to find the value that you're creating. Make it easy for them to fall in love with you, by communicating with them effectively, building a relationship with them, sharing your creations with them, and letting them know what you have to offer.

I love the fact that the Internet means that you no longer need to have ridiculous amounts of money to advertise on TV, radio, or in magazines and newspapers. You no longer need to have amazing connections to get you media coverage to get you in front of your audience. Now, you can leverage the power of the Internet – most of the time for free – to get yourself out there.

It's not a question of if you can do this, it's a question of how are you going to do it? So, let's make a plan for that right now…

Network Like Crazy

When I started FEA, no one knew who I was; no one knew that FEA even existed, so I had to figure out how to get it out there in front of my audience. How the heck was I going to build my platform?!

I realized that I had to go out there and start connecting with like-minded people and people within my audience. So I opened up my laptop and Googled, 'Business networking events.'

A huge list came up, and I had no idea whether the events would be good or bad, but I was going to find out!

The day of the first event came around, and there was a huge part of me that wanted to bail. I didn't know anyone and leaving the comfort of my home seemed like a lot of effort. But I was determined, so I ignored the Negative Committee and went along.

The event was a little awkward, but I met some lovely people, shared my plans for FEA, and asked people if I could share their story with my community, and for the first time, strangers knew about FEA and wanted to be part of it.

After that first event, I discovered more networking events and I made it my goal to go along to as many as possible because the more I got myself out there, the more I felt like momentum began to build.

I was making lots of wonderful new friendships with inspiring people and learning so much from them. Plus, I had the opportunity to hone my message because every time I went along to an event, I had to stand up in front of everyone and say who I was and what I did. I was growing, and FEA was growing. I felt like I was making a web of connections for FEA and getting the message out there.

The more I got out there, the more people I met who'd say, 'Oh have you heard of this event? You need to come along!' or 'Let me introduce you to this person, they'd love what you're doing!'

At one of these events, I met Lyndsey Meredith, who ran some networking events I'd attended, and we became friends, and she gave me the idea of finding groups of female entrepreneurs on LinkedIn.

Such a simple idea, but I hadn't thought to do it. Within a few days, I'd connected with hundreds of female entrepreneurs, and I was interacting in the groups, getting to know everyone. Then, I posted out a message to share that I was looking to publish stories about female entrepreneurs on my website. I invited anyone who was interested in sharing her story to click on the link I attached.

I hadn't anticipated much of a response, so when I checked later and found 15 replies from women not only in the UK but the USA, Canada, Hong Kong, and Nigeria, I was blown away.

FEA was no longer just an idea in my head but something that existed beyond me that women from all over the world were loving and getting involved with.

After a few months, I decided to set up a LinkedIn group for my audience. Because I'd been networking and building relationships with people, I had over 100 members join in the first 24 hours.

By this point, I also had my email list set up, using MailChimp – it was free – so I was driving traffic to the website, where people could sign up for my email list. Right there, on the home page, it said:

Join >> Share >> Connect >> Register.

*Becoming a member takes less than three minutes and it's free.
All you need to do is click the 'register' button at the top of the
page. Once you're a member you will be invited to have your story
published on FEA and you can build a profile and get involved in all
the great stuff going on here.*

Women were signing up, they wanted to get involved. I was building the
FEA platform.

I realized that getting myself out there and spreading my message wasn't
really that difficult, at all. Sure, it took a lot of effort and was pretty
exhausting, but once I started to weave my web, opportunities that I
could never have foreseen started to arise, and ideas I would never have
thought of started to come to me.

I was on a mission to do all I could to expand the reach of FEA.

SHE TAKES ACTION

What could you do to start connecting more with your audience
and getting your message out there? Research events you can go to,
online groups you could join, conferences to attend.

Get out there and start connecting.

Thank You, Facebook

I then began to focus on connecting with my audience and building my presence online, because I knew I wanted to reach women from all over the world, and I wouldn't find them at local networking events.

However, instead of trying to do everything, I decided to focus on getting really good at expanding my reach on Facebook. For me, it seemed to be the best platform, because I could share way more on Facebook than I could on Twitter and it resonated with me more than LinkedIn did, which felt quite corporate. So, I focused on sharing amazing content on Facebook that would communicate my message and resonate with my fans, in the hopes that they would want to like it, share it, and spread the message of FEA. I decided that I was going to be a Facebook master and figure out how I could get it to work really well for me. So I learned all I could and I began posting out and testing and testing and testing.

It began to work! People eventually started liking and sharing my content, I was getting more traffic to my website and my subscribers were growing. Then, through my pursuit of becoming a whizz on Facebook, I discovered Facebook Ads and decided to test them out to see if I could get in front of even more of my audience.

Google AdWords was my primary marketing strategy for building my first business, but this time I decided to use Facebook Ads because they would allow me to target women who owned a business and were fans of similar fan pages to mine – these were the people I really wanted to get in front of.

My goal was to create an advert using an inspirational quote to get more fans on Facebook, and then I wanted to nurture those fans with great content and blog posts, to drive them to the website, where they could find out more about FEA and sign up for the email list.

I had a spending limit of $10 a day for the ads, and within a month, I had 4,000 new fans! I couldn't believe it! Engagement shot up, traffic to my website increased, email subscribers increased. I was onto a winner… because I was using Facebook's clever targeting to get in front of women from English-speaking countries who were running their own businesses. Perfect.

Once I had a formula that worked, I focused my energy on getting better and better at leveraging it…

- I created valuable content.

- I shared it with my audience via Facebook, email and my website (making it compelling and sharable, so existing fans and subscribers would likely tell others about it and help me reach even more people).

- I expanded my reach by advertising on Facebook.

I then did this on rinse and repeat for other aspects of my business, too:

For my magazine:

- I created my free magazine (valuable content).

- I shared it with my audience via Facebook and my website.

- I created Facebook Ads to get it in front of more of my audience and people who weren't yet part of FEA.

For my live workshops:

- I began partnering up with amazing experts to host live workshops online, where they came to teach their strategies to my audience.

- I shared the upcoming workshop with my audience via Facebook and my website.

- I created Facebook Ads to make sure even more people knew that I was hosting it, so they could sign up and join us.

For my weekly videos:

- I create my weekly videos.

- I share them with my audience via Facebook, email and my website.

- I advertise my videos on Facebook, so more people will see them.

I could go on and on, but my point is that I've kept my marketing strategy simple, so that it is doable and so that I can become more and more effective at doing it.

I leverage the power of the Internet and Facebook to expand my reach far and wide, and that's how FEA has grown from nothing to a network of over 300,000, and over 4,000 amazing customers in the Members' Club.

You too have so much power in your computer to get you out there in front of your audience. All you need to do is find your magic formula. Here's how...

Finding Your Magic Formula

For FEA, Facebook and Facebook Ads have by far been my magic formula. It's got my little idea out there in front of *millions* of my dream audience, and for that I'm incredibly grateful. But Facebook isn't necessarily everyone's magic formula.

Michelle's magic formula is creating printables every month, which she gets in front of her audience using Pinterest. She realized that most people use Pinterest as a way to gather ideas and inspiration for improving different aspects of their lives, and this drives traffic to her website and builds her email subscribers.

She's also created paid printables, which she sells on Etsy. Her most popular printable is a kit called *The Ultimate Life Binder*, which helps people take 100 percent responsibility for their lives. She released the first edition of this product for $21 and it immediately started bringing in $1,000 a month in passive income, because people on Pinterest were discovering her pins about it and buying it. After a few months, that monthly income started climbing higher and after one year, Michelle's *Ultimate Life Binder* had generated over $20,000 in passive income! Her main source of traffic was Pinterest, which at the time had sent her over 100,000 views.

All she does is create very intentionally designed graphics to pin. To see an example go to http://bit.ly/SMB-Resources

In the example you see the following:

- A beautiful, bold headline.

- A sneak peek of what's inside the binder.

- A 'Click here' button, to get people to take action.

It's also a very long pin, so it stands out in the feed. This image has been pinned thousands and thousands of times, and every day, it's working its magic for Michelle.

That being said, business wasn't always this magical for Michelle. But she was determined to get her printables out there, making a difference, and making money. She took time to learn how to create higher converting pins, and she then kept testing and testing and testing. Six months later, the compound effect of people repinning her pins hit a tipping point, and the traffic to her Etsy store exploded.

This reinforces the point that we all have to keep testing and tweaking what we're doing in order to grow our businesses and get in front of our target audience.

Like FEA, Sam's magic formula for her wedding stationery business has been Facebook Ads.

In 2015, she set about to grow her wedding stationery business, and most of her focus was on creating beautiful collections that her brides would love. As the year went by, she attended a few wedding fairs and set up a gorgeous website. She even had a professional photo shoot to get amazing pictures of her work, so she could showcase her collections well online.

But as 2015 was drawing to a close, she began to feel disheartened and told me that she'd been feeling like a failure, because she realized that she hadn't really grown her business much at all in terms of revenue.

As 2016 rolled around, she made a decision that she was going to get her beautiful creations out there and take her business to another level, and so she decided to focus on Facebook Ads, having seen them work so well for FEA. So there I was sat in a cafe in London on a work trip, with my noodles and my laptop, and my phone started ringing. It was Sam, 'Right, I'm in the Facebook Power Editor, what do I need to do to get my ads up and running?'

I ate my noodles and walked her through how to use the Power Editor – showing her how to advertise to women within a certain age range, whose relationship status was 'engaged,' who lived in the UK, and who were fans of specific wedding blogs that were similar to her style. About 10 calls later, she'd uploaded her ads and they'd been approved!

Two days later, I got an excited text from her saying she'd sold her first sample, thanks to her ads. Within a month, she'd sold 17 samples and had eight new clients on board.

She said to me, 'Now I realize that last year was about preparing myself for this one. I needed to create my collections, get my online shop ready, and get beautiful pictures taken. Now, I've done that. This year, I can get it all out there in front of English brides and grow The Little Green Studio.'

When Kimra started doing her webinars, guess what she used to tell everyone about it? Facebook. She used Facebook Ads and Facebook groups to get her message out into the world.

When Nikki was starting her business in 2013, she used Facebook groups as a way to connect and communicate with her audience. She didn't have any products or services, yet, but she knew how she could add value and she knew who her audience were, so all she needed to do next was start communicating her value to her audience.

At the time, she was a member in a few Facebook groups for entrepreneurs. Some of them had a few hundred people, and others had a few thousand people. All she did was show up in the groups and be of service in any way she could. She was there to comment on people's posts, to cheer people on, to offer help if she could, and to just build relationships with the people there. She wanted to get to know them and she wanted them to get to know her.

Eventually, she created a survey so that she could find out specifically what entrepreneurs wanted help with when it came to communication. As a way of thanking the people for taking the survey, she said, 'I'm going to have 10 spots where I'll give away a free 30-minute session.'

She ended up getting 36 submissions of the survey and then ended up hosting 24 free sessions (on her days off, because she was still working). Doing those free sessions not only boosted her confidence in her abilities to really add massive value to people, but it also quickly led to her first paying customers and dozens of powerful testimonials.

All it took was her showing up in Facebook groups where her audience were already hanging out, and being there to build genuine relationships and clearly communicate her value.

There are over one billion users on Facebook, so you're bound to find your dream audience hanging out on there.

It's incredible how small the world has become, thanks to the Internet. I have the most incredible friends from all over the world because we've connected in online communities.

SHE TAKES ACTION

Finding communities online (and offline), where you'll find your audience hanging out, is so powerful. Truly become a part of these groups, by making it your goal to build wonderful friendships and connect deeply with the people in them. Do what you can to be helpful in the groups, to support the other members, and to serve them to the best of your abilities. People will respond.

If you don't know where to start, first run a search for groups on Facebook, and request to join a few. If you're looking to hang out with female entrepreneurs, come and join the 4,000+ people in our Facebook group!

Get out there, and make the most of it!

But don't overwhelm yourself. Get laser focused – pick ONE platform to leverage.

Having so many social media options is amazing, but can also lead to you feeling totally overwhelmed if you don't have a clear focus and a plan for how you're going to leverage social media to get your business and message out there.

I remember having a call with someone once and she was so overwhelmed, because she was trying to be on Facebook, Twitter, Pinterest, Instagram, and Periscope.

I get it. There is such a huge temptation to want to do it all, because you feel like if you don't try and do it, somehow you'll miss out. But when you attempt to do everything, it can be hard to keep all of the plates spinning, to keep up.

Social media management tools definitely help, but, ultimately, you need to be putting really amazing content out there. So, the best thing is to focus on getting really good at doing ONE thing first.

It's a bit like playing an instrument. You wouldn't decide to learn the clarinet, the piano, the saxophone, and the drums all at the same time!

You'd never get anywhere with it. Why try the same thing with so many social media platforms?

Give yourself permission not to have to do it all.

Allow yourself to focus on really leveraging one platform at a time. I'm not saying to ignore everything else completely – you can still link accounts and post on other platforms – I'm just saying pick a focus. Once you become amazing at leveraging that platform then, sure, you can look at focusing on another.

SHE TAKES ACTION

Think about where your audience hangs out, where you can communicate and engage with them the most, and where you can create the kind of content you like to create.

What you choose is not set in stone. You can always try new things, but get completely clear on what your #1 strategy is for getting yourself out there right now.

So what will your core marketing strategy be? Get clear on it, write it down, commit to becoming amazing at it, and focus your efforts on it.

Once you know what your core marketing strategy is, decide how much you're going to focus your time on it. Will you be focusing on working on your marketing and growth strategy once a week? One day a week? One hour a day? More than one hour a day?

If you decide to spend a set amount of time dedicated to your core marketing strategy and how you can make it more effective, you'll grow faster. When I was starting out and trying to figure out how I could make Facebook work for me, I was working on Facebook for hours a day. I was so committed to figuring it out. I was obsessed. Become obsessed with your marketing and growth.

Make the decision and stick to it.

When you focus on becoming amazing at one thing at a time, that's when the breakthroughs happen. That's when you reach the tipping point.

STEP 5: LET'S TALK ABOUT THE MONEY

Move Past Your Money Blocks

Having an amazing idea, creating wonderful things, getting yourself out there is all well and good, but at some point you have to receive as well as give.

I know so many women who love what they do so much, they want to give, give, give, and they forget to receive.

This is what happened to me for a long time.

I started my first business with the intention of making money, and I ended up making a lot of it, but after a few years, I felt empty. I wasn't passionate about what I was doing and, as I described earlier, set out to spend my life doing something I loved.

A few years later, when I started FEA, I was totally in love with what I was doing, but the reality was that it wasn't financially sustainable. I wasn't doing anything to generate revenue; all I wanted to do was give and ask for nothing in return. I did, however, know that I was on the right path and that if I could build a big audience of people who loved what I was doing, I could make it a huge success. The problem was that doubt clouded my mind and I got to the point where I felt like it was all hopeless. I wondered whether I'd ever be able to make it financially sustainable. In fact, I wrote in my journal on February 2:

'The money issue puts pressure on everything, to the point where you feel so crap and worried, you want to give up – but if money wasn't in the equation EVERYTHING right now would be fine!'

One day, just before Christmas in 2012, I hit rock bottom with it all. I didn't have any money to buy my family presents, and I knew I had to figure out how to make FEA sustainable. I realized that I had a number of money blocks – thoughts and feelings that I didn't need money or that I would never be able to make the money I desired, and it was stopping the flow of abundance into my life. So I took action to overcome them.

I called up my friend, Jason Jackman, and asked for some advice. He suggested I listened to visualizations to help me condition myself to open up and allow money to flow to me and then said, 'Carrie, the most powerful voice you can listen to is your own, so make your own visualization.' I had no idea how to do this, so we got together for the day, and he taught me how.

When I got home that evening, I wrote out a script and included lots of financial abundance affirmations in it that I resonated with. I Googled the best way to make an audio recording, and then I recorded my own financial abundance visualization.

As I fell asleep that first night listening to it, I made the decision that I was going to open up the gates and let money flow to me. When we commit to change, miraculous things can happen and that's exactly what happened to me when I committed to changing my money story...

A couple of days later I was looking through my emails and spotted one from a guy called Lewis Howes, someone I followed online. I'd been on his email list for a while, but hardly ever opened his emails, mainly because my inbox was so full and I was always too busy.

For some reason, though, I decided to open the one I saw. I read the email and then clicked through to the article he'd written, read the article, and then for some reason scrolled through the comments – something I never did! And there, in the comments, was a question someone had asked, and Lewis had replied, leaving his email address for the guy to get in touch.

In that moment, I knew I had to email him and see if there was anything I could do to support him. I'd listened to his webinars in the past and even bought one of his online training courses. I loved the value he offered, so I thought maybe I could promote his trainings to my audience – also something I'd never done before.

Without thinking twice I sent him the email, saying:

> Hey Lewis,
>
> I just wanted to get in touch to say I love what you guys do!
>
> I run the Female Entrepreneur Association, if there's anything I can do to support you, let me know.
>
> Carrie

That evening while I was out having dinner and drinks, I checked my phone to see if I had a reply, and I nearly fell off my chair when I saw that I did!! He said he'd love for me to host a webinar and he put me in touch with his business partner at the time to get it all set up.

Within a matter of days, we'd agreed that I was going to host a webinar with Amy Porterfield all about Facebook marketing. She had an online program called 'FB Influence,' and she would promote that at the end for anyone who wanted to carry on learning more. She sold it for $97 and for each one we sold I'd get 50 percent. I'd listened to Amy's webinars before and loved them, so when I found out I'd be hosting a webinar with her, I felt so nervous! But I knew I had to do it.

The webinar was set for December 20 and I thought hardly anyone would sign up for it, but I was wrong. We had over 1,000 sign-ups (because I was promoting it like crazy to my email list and Facebook audience), and a good few hundred people showed up live. I ended up making over $2,000 from that webinar.

Right then I realized that I had been denying my audience more value because I wasn't offering more. They loved the webinar, and the people who bought the program loved that, too. My money blocks began to dissolve, and I realized that it was OK for me to receive. In fact, the more FEA could receive, the more effective it would become at inspiring and empowering the women in my audience to build successful businesses. So the next year, I hosted more webinars with amazing people. In one of them, we made over $20,000! It blew my mind.

Then, I focused all of my energy on the best way to create a product or service of my own, for my audience. I had to work hard to move past the little voice that kept saying, 'You're not going to be able to do this!' But I was absolutely determined to figure it all out and by the end of 2013, I'd finally created the Members' Club. It wasn't perfect, I didn't have all the answers, I didn't know how it was all going to work out, but I'd done as much research as possible in or order to create a beautiful membership site and I got clear on what my offer was and how much I was going to charge.

Figuring out how much I was going to charge was a challenge. I went around in circles trying to decide. I desperately wanted to go into the future and find out what people would pay! I didn't want to undervalue myself, but I didn't want to overcharge and find myself struggling for members either. In the end I decided to stop listening to what everyone else was telling me and start tuning in more with my business and my vision for it all. I'd always wanted to help as many female entrepreneurs as possible, so I knew I wanted it to be affordable. That in itself helped guide my decision and it felt right, so I set the price at $25 per month and knew I could increase the price as the membership developed.

The biggest lesson I learned is that no one really knows 100 percent what price they should charge, so all you can do is go with what aligns best with your business and feels good to you. Once you've got your product or service out there, you can always adjust the price as things develop… your inner knowing will tell you when it's time, so listen out for it. I always get a feeling in the pit of my stomach when I think of the price and it leaves me feeling like it's not quite right. It's like a little siren going off telling me, 'It's time to increase the price.' I always listen to it.

Within a year, FEA's Members' Club had over 1,400 members and FEA had revenue of roughly $30,000 per month. I was ecstatic! I'd proved to myself that incredible things were possible, so the next year I set out to go from 1,000 members to 3,000 members. I had no idea how I was going to do it, but I believed with every cell in my body that I could – I knew I had to focus on adding lots of value, getting in front of my audience in a bigger way and offering them the chance to join the Members' Club, through well-thought-out launches. As that year closed out we had over 3,000 members.

When you smash through your money blocks it's amazing what you can achieve.

When I started FEA, I knew in my heart that if I could help enough other people, if I could build a big audience, and if I could establish FEA as the place to go for female entrepreneurs, the money would come. I knew that what I would have created would be incredibly valuable.

Throughout the journey, there have been times when I've questioned what I'm doing and times when I've wondered if I'll ever be able to make it work, but I've always kept the faith just enough to keep going.

SHE TAKES ACTION

Here are three things to help you move past your money blocks:

1. **Get clear on your money blocks** *by answering this question, 'What thoughts do I have around my ability/decision to make more money?' Write out all of your money beliefs and thoughts. Once you're clear on what's going on inside of your head, surrender them. Let them go, and start to open yourself. Be willing to allow more money into your life.*

2. **Reprogram your mind** *so that you can really align yourself with receiving what you want. I did this through inundating myself with financial abundance affirmations, reading books, and making a financial abundance guided visualization – I've created a script you can use to record yours – download it at http://bit.ly/SMB-Resources. Once you've recorded your visualization, listen to it daily before going to sleep, and really start to feel yourself opening up to receiving more. You can also access my abundance visualization on the link above too.*

3. **Take the right action.** *The last part of the jigsaw puzzle to financial abundance that got me to where I wanted to be was action – specifically, taking the right action. When opportunities came up I pounced on them, even when I was terrified. I wasn't where I wanted to be financially because I was taking the wrong action. I was doing things that were never going to get me to where I wanted to be, so I had to figure out what action I could take that would transform my situation. So, if what you're doing now isn't working, then what other action could you take?*

How Are You Going to Make Money?

The money piece is different for every one of us. I've interviewed hundreds of people and found that some of them have started a business and known exactly how they're going to make money, while others have had an overwhelming desire to create something, but no clue how the money would come.

When Sam followed her passion to learn about graphic design, she knew she'd ultimately be able to make money because people would hire her, but she didn't know how that would come about or what services she'd offer when she set off on her entrepreneurial adventure.

When Nikki started her entrepreneurial journey, she had no idea where the money would come from and so began exploring and building relationships, offering up some free sessions, and then she found her first customer. I asked Nikki how she transitioned from offering free sessions to paid sessions. Her response is a perfect sum-up of starting a new online service-based business.

'It was wildly simple because I had my system down. I had a 100 percent attendance rate for my free sessions, which I credit largely to setting and communicating very clear expectations up front. As soon as people signed up, I would send them a PDF with an overview that laid out exactly what they could expect before, during, and after our session — i.e. during the session, for the first five minutes, we'll do this, then we'll do this, and in the last five minutes, we'll do this. Two days after the session, I'm going to send you an eight-question survey to get your feedback.

I wanted to make sure they knew that up front I'd be following up with those Qs, because that was really what I wanted in exchange. The experience itself was great, but I wanted their feedback! Was it helpful? What was the best part for you? I'd be able to use that when I was ready to ask for money in exchange for it. Most of them replied to that survey, too.

'I had my system down. Next it was just a matter of how I was going to get paid for it. To save time going back and forth to schedule sessions, I set up a TimeTrade account. THEN I had to figure out how I was going to get paid. And I was very tempted to freak out about it. I remember writing on Jenny Shih's blog (she's a business coach and she's fabulous, now she's a good friend of mine but at the time I didn't know her, I just really loved her stuff). I thought, OK, let me ask Jenny. What do I need to do?

'I left a comment saying something like, "I need to get started but I don't know how to get paid. I don't know what my tax structure is going to be: LLC versus blah-blah-blah."

'She replied (and I joke that it was like an e-slap in the face, where it's like somebody throws water in your face and they're like "Pull yourself together, man!") – she was like, "Nikki, this is a case of making something a thousand times harder than it needs to be. Just get a PayPal link and you'll figure it all out before tax season next April," which was a year away.

'I was like, "Oh, OK. RIGHT.' I created a PayPal link and I was officially ready to accept payments."

'Next I had to tell people about my offer! I had all these testimonials from my free sessions, so I posted them in the Facebook groups I was in and I told everyone, "OK, I'm going to have an offer for you starting tomorrow."

'Thing is, I didn't know what the offer was going to be, even when I posted that. That was on a Monday, and I remember talking with my sister Stacey on the phone, asking her, "What should my offer be?"

'She was like, "I don't know." We decided I would offer one-hour sessions for $199 and a bonus of a 30-minute follow-up session. At the time, I didn't have a website. I had Nikkielledgebrown.com, which was just a splash page with an opt-in box. It wasn't even a cute splash page, it was just: "Here's what's going to be coming up." I posted about it in the Facebook groups and then people could go opt in to see what the heck I was talking about. It was crazy from there.

Over the course of that 10-day period when I was offering the 30-minute bonus session, 70 people took me up on it – SEVENTY! It was like a perfect storm, because I was helping people with their communication skills, but I was also modeling my own communication skills so they could literally see, "Oh, she knows what she's talking about, and I like her. She doesn't feel sales-y to me. She's communicating her message. I feel like I know her." I didn't have a video up on the website. I literally had a cropped maternity photo and a makeshift logo I had made in PowerPoint up on my site. That was that. Shows the power of clear, sincere communication!

'In the email that I sent to people once they opted in, it was basically an email version of the "what to expect" PDF I used for the free sessions, with more info to make it clear, i.e. "If this is your problem, I can help. Here's how I can help. Here's exactly what to expect and here's how to take me up on it." (Not the exact words, but the main idea!)'

And they did take Nikki up on her sessions! She started booking one-hour sessions at $199 immediately and with a rapid increase in demand (and testimonials) was able to increase her prices from there.

There are a few amazing messages I'd like to highlight from Nikki's story:

- You don't have to have it all figured out! You need to take the action and then let the pieces fall into place.

- You don't need to have everything set up and in perfect order. She didn't have a full-blown website when she started. She had a process for communicating her message, her value, and how she could help her audience.

- She didn't stall, trying to figure it all out by herself. She asked for help. Do you know how much time people waste trying to figure out online payments, because they overcomplicate it?!

- She took it all one step at a time. She did free sessions first, because that's what she felt was the right next step for her to take. From there, the path quickly opened up and she realized how she could start generating revenue.

That year, she did so many one-on-one sessions and learned so much from doing it that she created an online program so she could teach her strategies to even more people. In her first 10 months of business, Nikki made over $100k.

All it took was getting started and keeping on going.

Michelle saw a similar pattern. She started her blog, 'The Secret O.W.L. Society,' with absolutely no idea how she was going to make money from it, but she went on the adventure with an open mind and turned her blog into a profitable business.

'I never thought that I would make money with the blog but as I was building it and learning as much as I could, I discovered Pinterest. It was then that I was exposed to people who were making money blogging. All of a sudden, I started thinking about how I could I too.

'Turning the blog into a business came down to having you [Carrie]

as a mentor. I was working with you, and I could see everything you were doing, "Wow, she's taking this idea and look at how she's turning it into an empire." It was a process of just slowly implementing little things in order for it to become more of a business. Part of that was doing what you were telling me to do. I had the blog for three years and I didn't collect a single email. I think you asked me three times in a row, "Did you start your MailChimp yet?" No, I didn't.

'That was a turning point, because now I was writing emails to hundreds of people, "What am I going to email them about?" I started to think about what I had to offer them. What do they expect from me? What can I be regularly giving them that they expect me to be consistent at giving them? As I became better at printables that's when I realized, 'Wow, I could create printables that people really love. I know I can create some of this stuff and people will download it.

'I remember sending out a survey asking people what they wanted me to create. That was another turning point for me, thinking, I can create an income here. I can turn this into a business, because people are telling me, "We want you to add more printables to your Etsy store. We want you to start a members' club. We want you to create a life binder that we can buy."

'I think the reason why I never thought of my blog as a business was down to my mindset. I had to have a mindset shift where I realized, I can create something that people will buy. I didn't make that shift until I got all the responses from the survey saying, "We want to buy more stuff from you." At that point, I had one or two printables in the store. I was capable of creating this stuff, but I wasn't acting like people would care about buying it.

'So, I got myself on Fiverr, and I put up a service saying, "Hey, I'll create a printable for you for $5." Doing that helped me because I started getting tons of people ordering printables. At that point, I was still creating everything on PicMonkey; I didn't even know how to use Google Docs, yet. I got so many orders, all of the customers were happy, but it got to a point where I couldn't keep up anymore and shut it down. It was a good thing because it helped me realize I could do it and make money at it. I realized that people loved my printables. So I began to grow the stock of printables in my Etsy store and it started making money.

'It wasn't until a while later, when I had the pressure of two trips coming up, that I started to focus more on generating more revenue. I knew I could save the money for the trips, but part of my philosophy was to find a way to challenge myself. I knew I didn't want to go on the trips and come home to less money. I had been to Europe before and I had been traveling to the States before, but everything had always had to stop while I took the trip. Then, you come home, and you have to restart. So, I knew I wanted to make money while I was traveling. I wanted to feel like a successful businessperson. I wanted to have that feeling of, "I'm going home soon, but I'm in a better position than when I left."

'That's what really compelled me to create my bestselling product, "The Ultimate Life Binder." I already knew people wanted it, because people told me in the survey that they really wanted it. So I created it and put it up on the store at a much higher price than any of my other printables. Almost right away, it started replacing my living expenses, and while I was traveling it kept making sales. In the beginning, it was $1,000 a month. Then, I was making around $2,000 a month on average. It even made as much as $4,000 in a single month. Month after month, the money keeps coming in.

'That was the whole journey. It was very organic. There were only a few things I did that enabled me to build my business. Creating my email list so I could communicate and engage with my audience, figuring out what one thing people found valuable, and just focusing on creating it and getting it out there.'

Imagine if at the beginning of Michelle's entrepreneurial adventure she'd given up, because she didn't know how the money would come?

Sometimes you just don't know how the money will come. Sometimes you doubt if it will come, but if you believe in your idea, if you're clear on your mission, if you know who your audience are, and if you get yourself in front of them, engaging with them, and communicate your value with them, you'll figure out a way to get the money to come.

SHE TAKES ACTION

Whether your business is already generating revenue or not, take some time to think about what you want your money story to look like. Get clear on your money goals and then work backward and ask yourself, 'What can I do right now to start generating this revenue?' Open up your mind and start exploring the possibilities.

Use the following affirmation as often as you need to help you overcome any blocks you have toward receiving financial gain.

'Money flows to me quickly and easily.'

I am financially abundant. Money flows to me quickly and easily.

YOUR GROWTH
GAME PLAN

Building a successful business is something we can all do, although most of the time the journey feels messy and chaotic! So to help you feel organized and focused about the steps you need to take in order to up-level your business and turn it into a success, use the questions below to map out your business growth game plan.

You can download the fill-in worksheet version at http://bit.ly/SMB Resources

Your mission

- What's your personal mission for starting your business? Why are you doing it?

- What's your business mission? Sum it up in one simple sentence.

- What does your business stand for? What are its beliefs and values?

Your audience

- Who are you serving?

- Who do you want to listen to your message?

- Who will your message appeal to?

Engaging your audience

- How will you delight your audience?

- How do you want to make them feel?

- What experience do you want to create for them?

(Remember, you don't have to have it all figured out!)

Expressing your brand

- What fonts and colors do you want to use?

- What's your design style?

- How will you align your brand with your message and resonate with your audience?

Serving your audience

- How will you go above and beyond to serve your audience?

- What will you offer them?

- How will you engage with them?

- What challenges/frustrations are they facing that you could solve?

- What could you create that they would LOVE *and resonate with*?

- How will you add value?

Getting in front of your audience

- How will you get your business and message out there in front of your audience?

- How will you get noticed?

- How will you build a fan base?

- What is going to be your core focus?

- How will you build authority, credibility, and trust?

Ultimately, there are so many ways to get out there in front of your audience and figuring out what will work for you is an exploration, so go along for the ride and see for yourself what will work best.

Your goals and plan for the next six months

- What do you want to achieve over the next six months?

- How are you going to make this happen?

- What is your plan for growth?

Getting started plan

What action do you need to take right away in order to get the ball rolling?

For example:

- Deciding on a name.

- Buying a domain name.

- Setting up your website hosting.

- Building your website.

- Setting up an online shop.

- Setting up your Facebook fan page.

- Setting up your Instagram account.

- Setting up a Pinterest account.

- Setting up a podcast or videos series and planning out content and when you'll record them.

- Creating a content schedule for social media and the blog.

- Creating any free content you'll use to get more email subscribers and for that matter, setting up your email host so you can actually get subscribers.

- Researching what Facebook groups you could join and the fan pages where you could advertise.

- Setting deadlines for when each action has to be completed.

Ultimately, this whole process is about getting clear on the possible things that *could* work. You don't have to have all the answers, you don't need to know 100 percent what will work and what won't, but what you do need to do is explore the options and do your best to get your business out in front of your audience.

You can achieve spectacular things when you put your mind to it and work for it.

Business success is not limited to a special few.
Business success is not an accident.
It's yours for the taking, if you commit to it.

You can do it – let your intuition guide you.

'Don't wait.
The time will
never be
just right.'

Napoleon Hill

BE RELENTLESS

'You can have results or excuses. Not both.'
ARNOLD SCHWARZENEGGER

Throughout my entrepreneurial journey, hard work and me have become best friends, especially when I was just starting out.

I worked tirelessly on turning my idea into a successful reality. Quite often I'd be at my laptop working at 8 a.m. and still sitting there at 2 a.m. My back would ache, my eyes would be tired, but my mind would be racing.

It was as if my laptop was an extension of my body, because it went everywhere with me. I was relentless and obsessed by getting to where I wanted. I slogged away day in, day out to turn my idea into reality, trying to figure out how to make it work, constantly working on applying the strategies I've shared with you in this section. Always asking, 'How can I make this the best platform for women ever? How can I serve my audience even better?'

Ultimately, it's the entrepreneurs who put in the work and consistently take action that succeed, because you can't have the results if you don't put in the effort. It's that simple.

The best part is that we can all be that person – the person who's prepared to work tirelessly in order to succeed.

Maybe you can't work all hours of the day, but you can become so consumed and obsessed with the idea of succeeding that you spend every moment you possibly can on working toward building your business.

There are no business fairies that can do the work for us (although that would be nice!). We have to step up and do the work.

If you want to make something happen badly enough, you will put in the work to make it happen, no ifs, ands, or buts.

Once your hard work starts to pay off (you have to trust that it will) you'll be able to reap the rewards of your labor.

I remember a couple of years ago I was in Yosemite National Park for my sister's wedding and we'd all hired bikes and were cycling through the valley. I had the breeze in my hair and the most breathtakingly beautiful view surrounding me and I remember thinking, 'Wow, I'm living my dream.'

There I was enjoying living life, while my business was generating revenue without me having to do anything.

All of my hard work over the years has well and truly paid off and now I get to enjoy living the life I dreamed of. Let me tell you, the hard work will be worth it.

So roll up your sleeves and be prepared to step up and work your butt off and give it your all in the pursuit of creating a wildly successful business.

MOVING PAST
COMPARISONITIS

'Don't compare your Chapter 1 to someone else's Chapter 20.'
UNKNOWN

There are a lot of amazing people out there, doing amazing things, and they inspire us. But sometimes they can also trip us up, if we're not careful, because we get sucked into their amazingness, and forget about our own.

We think we should be more like them and do things the way they do things.

This can have a twofold effect:

1. We start to doubt ourselves. We think we're nowhere near as good and never will be.

2. We think that it's all hopeless and who the heck are we to do what we're doing?

We start to think that our only option is to be more like that person, and so we chip away at our own style, our own uniqueness, to be more like someone else. This causes us to lose our authenticity and disconnect from who we truly are.

It also leaves us feeling terrible.

The reason we experience this comparisonitis is because we are human beings. Smile. You're not alone. It's all OK.

That said, don't let someone else dull your shine, rise up and shine with them by taking action to stop comparisonitis holding you back or derailing your plans.

SHE TAKES ACTION

Stop being obsessed with everyone else for a little while by taking a break from anyone who makes you feel inferior, anyone who you keep comparing yourself to, anyone who makes you feel bad, because what they do makes you feel like you'll never be as good.

Then, focus on being the best you can be by writing down why you're amazing. Write down your achievements – the big, the small, and the teeny tiny. Write down how you intend to rise up and be even more glorious than before.

Whenever you realize that you're comparing yourself to someone else, say, 'Stop' to yourself, and think of something that makes you feel good. This will change your thinking to be more positive, and – as we talked about in Part 1 (see page 56) – positive thinking leads to powerful action.

You might also like to use the following affirmation to help keep you on track or for those times when you start comparing yourself to others:

'I am unique and special. I love and approve myself.'

CONNECTING THE DOTS
GOING BACKWARD

'You can't connect the dots looking forward. You can only connect them looking backward. So you have to trust that the dots will somehow connect in your future.'
STEVE JOBS

Looking back on my journey of building FEA, I can clearly see the path I took, which, in short, looks like this:

- I got clear on my mission – on what FEA was really about and what the values of the business are.

- I've worked to consistently get to know my audience better.

- I decided how I wanted to make my audience feel and what I could do to make them feel that way – inspired and empowered.

- I focused on how I was going to serve, delight and add value to my audience – I created content, freebies, the Members' Club and more.

- I decided how I was going to get in front of my audience, connect with them and invite them on my journey – mainly using Facebook.

- I've consistently worked to expand my reach, add value, build a deep relationship with my audience and communicate what I have to offer – I've done this on rinse and repeat.

Writing it out like this looks neat and straightforward, but that's because I'm connecting the dots looking backward. Don't get me wrong, these are the exact steps I have taken, and they're the steps that pretty much anyone building a successful business has taken, but when you're on the journey of implementing these steps, it doesn't always feel this simple.

When I was starting FEA, it felt overwhelming, complicated, and incredibly messy – and often still does. I wanted to have things figured out, but I didn't. I wanted to know exactly how I was going to build my big audience, but I didn't.

I didn't know how long it would take to build up my Facebook fan page, to get lots of email subscribers, to have a ton of traffic coming to my website, to start making money, or to get people commenting and engaging with my videos and posts.

But I knew that, somehow, I would make it work, because it felt right.

Ultimately, the steps we have to take are simple, but the same can't always be said for the journey.

My point is that every single one of us can take these steps, there's no question about that. However, the question is, will you be the person you need to be in order to keep taking them? When the road gets rough, when life gets in the way, when things feel hopeless, when everything is so chaotic you feel like you're losing your mind, will you keep going?

I want you to know that your tribe is out there waiting for you and hoping that you'll keep following through on the steps you need to take, even when it's frustrating, even when life gets in the way, even when it feels hopeless, even when you've fallen off the bandwagon and you feel like you just can't pull yourself back up.

I want you to know that YOU CAN.

You are stronger than you think. The universe is urging you to remember this, otherwise you wouldn't be reading these words at this very moment.

· THE CHECKLIST ·
She Gets Herself Out There to Shine

Here's a reminder of what you need in order to make the most of your ideas.

O Know what's at the heart and soul of your business. Your mission, your why, your values.

O Know who your audience are.

O Know how you're going to serve them.

O Know how you're going to get in front of them.

O Go above and beyond to delight them and create a wonderful experience for them.

O Take action consistently to grow and expand your tribe.

O Constantly engage with your audience.

O Be your authentic, amazing self and no one else.

O Get clear on your money story – what you want and how you'll make it happen.

O Be relentless in the pursuit of building a wildly successful business.

O Don't compare yourself with others.

O Keep it simple.

PART THREE

She's Unstoppable

HONOR THE PROCESS

The entrepreneurial journey pushes us to do things we've never done before. It forces us to dig into the depths of who we are, in order to show up and make stuff happen.

While there are times when we feel so excited, inspired, and fired up, there are also times when we feel like everything is ridiculously tough and impossible. It's all part of the process, and we need to honor it because there is no way around it. As much as you'd like, you can't skip the tough bits.

Those tough bits are there for a reason. They help you to fine-tune who you are, what you like and don't like, and what works for you. The more you get to know yourself, the more intuitive you become, which will be invaluable in helping you to navigate the way forward. Even when you feel really unsure, or downright miserable, know that you just have to keep moving forward in the direction of your dreams, and as you do, the only place you're going is upward.

That is such a liberating thought! To, me it feels like laughing in the face of discomfort and all of the other things that try to knock us off track, while saying, 'Thank you so much for coming to visit me, you're making me stronger.'

All of these things help to make us unstoppable, which is exactly what we have to be as entrepreneurs, because it's not the skill, the talent, or the good ideas that will help you to create the success you want – it's you.

The skill, the talent, and good ideas are born from the persistence, the determination, and the drive to succeed, not the other way around.

Over the years, I've found that there are specific things that have helped me to become unstoppable. These things have helped me to up-level and breakthrough and create the business I dreamed of, and I'd like to share them with you now, along with a few of my journal entries.

'She was unstoppable, not because she didn't have failures or doubts, but because she continued on despite them.'

Beau Taplin

YOU'VE GOT TO HAVE PERSISTENCE

'Last week I was feeling crappy that things have been going so slow – but I guess it's going to be hard. I was talking to my friend about it and I realized that we really do choose to sink or swim – I actually find this really empowering – that we can choose.'

MY JOURNAL, OCTOBER 6, 2011

When I started FEA, I didn't really think about how long it would take me to turn my idea into reality, I just knew that I was on a mission to make it happen, no matter how long it took.

That being said, there were so many times when I felt completely put off by how long it was actually taking! It made me question myself, 'Why is this taking so long? What is wrong with me?' At times, I felt like I was a crazy lady for keeping on going. There were times when people would say, 'Carrie, when are you going to go and get a proper job?' and I would think, 'I have enough doubts of my own, I don't need yours too!' Sometimes people who love you just can't see the same vision you do.

There were also times when I dreamed about quitting and going to get a mindless job so that I wouldn't have to worry whether I'd be able to 'make it happen' with FEA.

I think just about every entrepreneur has had the same thoughts, at some point or another. We live in a fast-paced world, and we want things to happen NOW.

But turning an idea into a successful reality takes time, usually a lot more time than you anticipate, even though you know your idea is amazing and you think people should snap it up right away! We entrepreneurs are all a bit delusional, but we kind of have to be! How long it takes is different for all of us. There's no right or wrong length because we're all on our own journey.

I spent the first two years focused entirely on building my audience, and it wasn't until my third year that I actually started to make decent money, and I was into my fourth year when FEA began making a significant amount of money.

Along my journey, I've seen people start businesses and make more money in the first few months than I made in the first three years. There were times when I beat myself up about it, but I also know that there are plenty of others who started their business before me and are still making less.

You know what? It doesn't matter, because everyone is on their own journey. As long as your focus point is, 'How can I grow? How can I improve? How can I make my business even more amazing and get it out there in front of my audience? How can I create a business and life I love?' then you are heading in the right direction, and nothing else matters.

So become the most persistent person you know and keep on going and going and going.

We have to keep walking our own path, keep writing our own story, & trust that, somehow, it will all unfold in the right way.

KEEPING THE FAITH

On many occasions I've had to talk myself into keeping the faith and carrying on. It's all too easy to feel discouraged, but it's in those moments that you have to dig deep and trust that somehow it will all work out as it's supposed to.

I once wrote in my journal:

> *'I feel like I'm flagging with the whole project. I'm not sure if it's because it's taking so long to get the site up or that I've reached a stage where I don't really know how I'm going to take it forward or which direction to take it or whether I'm just scared in case no one signs up.'*

AUGUST 16, 2011

There's a quote I love which says, 'Successful people hang on when everyone else has let go.' I printed it out and stuck it on my wall, where I could see it every day during the first few years of building FEA, because I needed to constantly remind myself to be the person that was prepared to hang on.

Be the person that's prepared to keep hanging on, because your trust runs so deep that you know things will work out.

I've already described how certain words are important to me (see page 63), and on my vision board is the word 'TRUST' in big letters.

Constantly remind yourself that you have to trust yourself, your vision, your business, your instincts, and the journey. You have to trust that somehow the ups and the downs are guiding you to where you need to go.

If you don't, then you'll go mad. You'll fight back, and you'll struggle even more than you need to. Relax, let go, take in a deep breath, and trust that what you want is a done deal and it's coming your way.

Abraham Hicks once gave a brilliant analogy for this. A person at one of their conferences stood up and said they were losing faith in ever reaching their goal. Abraham said that if you were going to drive from Phoenix to San Diego, with every mile you drove in the direction of San Diego, you'd know that you were a mile closer. Even if you hit traffic, even if things came to a complete standstill, even if you had to take a detour, you'd know with absolute certainty that you would, eventually, get to San Diego, because it's a physical journey.

See reaching your goals the same way. You have to know that with every step you take toward your goal it's a step closer. You have to know, with certainty, that despite the setbacks and challenges, if you keep facing forward and moving forward you will get there. It might take longer than you thought, or it might be quicker than you thought, but you will get there.

Since hearing this analogy, I have viewed all of my goals as a done deal. If I set the goal to go to San Diego, I know I could get there, so I know that if I set myself a non-physical goal I can get there too. It might take time, but I can get there.

When you shift your perspective to thinking of your journey like that, it helps to keep the faith and trust that what you want is a done deal, even if it feels hopeless at that given moment of time.

Do not be disheartened when it takes you more time that you'd like, you have to practice the art of persistence and faith – a winning combination in the pursuit of becoming unstoppable.

Keep walking your walk, and don't give in.

'Faith is like Wi-Fi. It's invisible but has the power to connect you to what you need.'

Unknown

YOU'VE GOT TO
PRACTICE LIKE CRAZY

*'I was chatting to Dad about the candle idea today and he said he'd
looked up the accounts for a big candle company and they made a loss
for the first couple of years. It's kind of good to know, because sometimes
it's easy to get carried away thinking you can start an idea and it will
be instantly amazing and profitable, but it doesn't work like that.'*
MY JOURNAL, DECEMBER 6, 2012

No one is born a genius entrepreneur. It doesn't just happen overnight –
as much as we'd like it to. It takes a lot of practice to create a profitable
business, and, even then, you have to practice your skills all the time.

I learned this lesson when I was a teenager. On my eighth birthday, I got
a clarinet. I was so excited about it. I opened the box, pieced it together,
and blew down the mouthpiece… nothing but a squeak came out.

I didn't know any notes, I didn't know how to do anything. I was
completely clueless – much like I was when I started my first business!
But I was determined to get good, and so, as you do when learning a
musical instrument, I got a clarinet teacher who began teaching me what
I needed to know. Then, I practiced and practiced and practiced.

I hated it.

I drove my dad and my teachers to despair because I hated practicing. I found it tedious and frustrating – playing the same scale over and over and over again and still not being able to play was beyond annoying.

There were times when all I wanted to do was throw my clarinet on the floor and quit. But I didn't. I just kept on practicing, and I got better and better. And within seven years, I'd passed Grade 8 and was playing Mozart's Clarinet Concerto.

I find it interesting that we all know that if we decided to learn to play an instrument, we'd be terrible at the beginning and then we'd have to learn new skills and practice those skills until we got to where we wanted to be. We all know that even when we did finally reach a certain level, we'd have to keep practicing to stay at that level and develop further.

So, why is it that when most people decide to start a business, they think they should be good right out of the gate, and know everything to the point where they either don't get help or just beat themselves up for not being good enough?

If you want to get good at anything you'll probably start off being terrible, and then when you take the time to learn and practice, you'll get better and better, no doubt about it.

Will it be easy? Probably not – especially at the beginning when you're feeling overwhelmed and frustrated about the tasks ahead and ready to quit!

But can you get good, amazing even? The answer is 100 percent YES!

If you dedicate yourself to practicing getting good at business, you'll get good at business.

If you dedicate yourself to learning how to build your audience, and you practice, practice, practice, you'll get good at it and you will actually build your audience, no ifs, ands, or buts.

If you dedicate yourself to getting good at running Facebook Ads to grow your business and you consistently practice, you'll get good at growing your business using Facebook Ads.

If you want to be successful, practice doing the things you need to do in order to be successful and you'll become unstoppable.

CONSISTENCY IS THE KEY

'I feel like I want to do so much stuff at the moment,
but I can't do it all. It's so frustrating!'
MY JOURNAL, SEPTEMBER 6, 2012

I am a huge ideas person; I think most entrepreneurs are. I come up with a new idea, get ridiculously excited, and then want to just drop everything and start working on that, right away.

Needless to say I've learned that I have to stop myself, make a note of my idea, and carry on with what I was originally doing, because success comes from what you do consistently.

Along my entrepreneurial journey, I've experienced an ongoing desire to jump from one idea or strategy to the next. I've definitely suffered with Shiny Object Syndrome, whether it's a new idea I've come up with or a new social media platform I want to try out – usually because I heard someone say that it was amazing and that everyone should be using it!

At times, I've found it difficult to hold back and stop myself from being distracted. There have been times when I've got so dazzled by the shiny object that I've caved and poured time and attention into it, only to realize that it took me off track.

When Periscope came out, people were raving about how it was the next best thing and that every entrepreneur had to be on there. I watched what people were doing for a while, with a mounting pressure that I should be broadcasting on Periscope, too. I felt like I was missing out somehow, so I caved and I started live streaming via Periscope.

I dedicated time to think of content for my live broadcasts, and I spent time actually doing the live broadcasts. As it was a new platform for me, I had no following, so I focused on building it up.

After a few months, people had already moved on to the next thing – Facebook Live – and in the end I stopped doing the live broadcasts.

I wouldn't go as far as to say I wasted my time because time can't be called wasted when you learned something from what you were doing. That being said, it did take me away from spending time on the platform I'd chosen to focus on to help me grow my business – Facebook.

It was a classic case of Shiny Object Syndrome.

Ultimately, there will be things we come across or ideas we come up with that are so tempting to pursue, but if we're not careful, we end up hopping from one idea/strategy to the next, which causes our progress to slow or stall entirely.

The key is to focus on one thing at a time and to be ridiculously consistent at becoming amazing at it.

When you put your focus and effort into being consistent at something, that's when the breakthroughs happen. That's when things start to fall into place.

Yes, there will be times when you want to pack it all in and try something else because you'll hit challenges and obstacles. Like I've said before, in the early days of building FEA I decided that I was going to focus on becoming amazing at Facebook. I knew that in order to do that I had to consistently put out new content, engage with others, and learn how I could grow my Facebook platform. But, at the beginning, it felt confusing, overwhelming, and disheartening. I'd create content, put it out there and get no likes or comments.

There was a huge part of me that thought, 'What's the point?' But I made a commitment to myself to be consistent and things started to happen that made me realize I was on the right path – whether it was a comment from a stranger, or an increase in fans – so I kept on going. As a result, my Facebook platform kept on growing.

Give yourself permission to keep it simple and to focus on one core thing. You don't have to be doing it all. In fact, trying to do it all is far less effective because it often leads to creating a tangled mess of nothing!

What are you going to focus on consistently? Make a commitment to it right now, and focus on it.

Now, just because you're committed to being consistent with one core focus doesn't mean to say that you're not still going to have a bazillion tasks to work on.

You will still be doing lots of things to run and grow your business, and that's exactly why you need to be extremely focused.

HOW TO AVOID
OVERWHELM

*'I had a look through a women's magazine over the
weekend, it was 56 pages and about 20 people put it
together! Here's me trying to create a monthly magazine
the same size all by myself!! Oh well, you only live once.'*

MY JOURNAL, MARCH 2, 2012

As I described earlier in the book, I began work on creating my
monthly magazine in 2012. Except for Natalie, my designer, I was
putting the entire thing together myself and bringing advertisers on
board, too.

People thought I was mad for attempting to pull it off. I thought I
was partially mad for trying to do it, too, but I was determined and I
was focused.

At the beginning, the excitement and adrenaline got me through, but by
month three, I felt like I was sinking. I had so many plates spinning. I was
responsible for coming up with the content, for doing interviews, for
reaching out to experts, writing articles, getting advertisers on board,
and for marketing the entire thing. I felt like I couldn't keep up.

I was overwhelmed and everything felt like one big mess. I needed to get a grip.

So, I called my friend Jason Jackman for help.

We met in London and spent the entire day sat in the lobby of a swanky London hotel talking business. He shared with me his strategy for reducing overwhelm and staying on track and focused. His strategy was called 'mini days,' and after going through it all with him, it made me feel like a weight had been lifted.

We met at around 11 a.m., and after ordering drinks and catching up, he asked me what had been going on. I began to tell him about the overwhelm I was experiencing – the words coming out of my mouth frantically, as if mirroring how I felt. My mind was spinning, I felt like I was so tangled up in my business I didn't know how to keep moving forward.

I finished with a deep breath, and felt relieved that I'd got out everything I'd wanted to say. Then, he told me everything would be OK and that I'd make it work, I just needed to break it all down.

So simple, yet I'd completely forgotten to do it, and I'd just been consumed with everything all in one go.

Over the next few hours, we dived into my business, and he asked me exactly what I was spending my time doing. We wrote it all out so that I could have a bird's-eye view of what I was doing with my time. It really put into perspective how manic and unfocused I'd become.

Then, he started asking me about my main focus, which at the time was my magazine and growing my audience.

He asked me to tell him the process for creating the magazine, something I'd never even consciously thought about before. I began by telling him that the first part was to work out what content would be going into the issue. He then got me to break down the magazine into sections, so I could see exactly what features went into each magazine:

- How She Did It interview

- Cover interview

- Personal development article

- Business article

- Ask and Answered

- 10 Things to Remember on Your Journey

- 5 Things to Try This Month

And so on.

Once we'd mapped out the content, he asked me how long it took me to create each piece and what steps were involved. For example, what the process was for the cover interview, editing the text, and preparing it for publication.

I began to think through it all and wrote down how long each step took me.

Then, we moved on to breaking down the next phase of the magazine, which was getting the advertisers on board. I wrote down the process and how long it all took me.

Then we moved to the next phase, which was design. As I wasn't responsible for this part, we mapped out how long the design usually took and what date I had to get it over to Natalie, so she could work on it and have it finished and ready to launch the following month.

Then the next phase was getting it live and marketing it – I mapped out exactly how I was marketing the magazine once it went live:

- Upload the magazine to the website and make sure the page is all good to go, with subscribe buttons to get people to sign up.

- Launch magazine at the beginning of each month.

- Send out email to entire network, letting them know the next issue is live.

- Create multiple graphics of the magazine to share on Facebook and then schedule them to go out throughout the entire month.

- Set up Facebook Ads to expand the reach and get more people reading the magazine.

- Monitor ads throughout the month.

I wrote out how long each task took me, and by the end of the analysis I realized that my life just got a whole lot easier! I actually had a process for creating the magazine. Now that I had a business map, I knew exactly how much time I should be spending on each activity – it was like I could finally see the wood for the trees. I was no longer in the tangled mess; I'd taken control and could see how every part of my business was operating. It was a massive relief.

But the strategy day didn't end there.

Next, he told me in order to make the most of my business map, I needed to stay in control and keep on track by creating mini days. So rather than seeing the entire day as one chunk with a to-do list of items, none of which have a beginning or end, you break your day into one-hour to two-hour chunks of time. For each chunk of time, you assign yourself one task to work on.

The trap I was falling into was letting one task take over an entire day or week, and then I'd get so far behind on everything else. For example, I'd be so consumed by creating content that I'd forget to focus on marketing and expanding my reach. Therefore, my business didn't grow as fast, and I felt like I was suffocating it.

At the beginning of your business, it's likely that you're the one who's doing practically everything, so you need to know how to work in an effective way so that you can make the progress you want, and mini days can really help you do just that.

As Jason was telling me about how mini days work, we began to put it all into practice. We started by categorizing my tasks:

- Writing content

- Doing interviews

- Getting advertisers on board

- Marketing

- Admin (emails)

- Finance

- Meetings/calls

- Miscellaneous

This is how I chose to break down my activities.

I color-coordinated each category, and then created a table in a Word document (I now use Google Calendar instead) that listed out the days of the week across the top and the time of my mini days down the side. I began to plot out what activities I was going to work on and when.

I worked out what recurring daily tasks I had, what recurring weekly tasks I had and what recurring tasks I had on a monthly, quarterly, and annual basis.

At the end I felt like I'd created my own business curriculum; I'd never felt so organized in my life.

Then, I plotted out the following week's mini days, and was able to review my very first business timetable. That one day with Jason changed my entire approach to running my business. He gave me the tools I needed to get organized and to stay focused – two massively important things we have to do as entrepreneurs.

As FEA grew and I began to get busier and busier, I was keen to learn more about creating systems and processes for my business activities. I wanted to turn FEA into a well-oiled machine, and in my quest to do just that I came across the lovely Natasha Vorompiova, founder of Systems Rock, and I was eager to see what I could learn from her. I quickly realized it was a lot.

One of the best things she's taught me is how to create my own business hub, the digital home of everything that goes on inside FEA.

I chose to create FEA's hub in Asana because it's free and I was able to create lists, projects, tasks, and templates so I could see exactly what was going on in my business.

The first thing I did was break down everything going on inside of FEA, which at the time, looked something like this:

- Website

- Members' Club

- Marketing, launching and outreach

- Admin

- Finance

Under each of those headings was everything going on inside each category; for example under 'website,' I listed:

- Motivation Monday post

- Tuesday Video post

- '5 Things to Try This Month' post

- 'How She Did It' daily post

- Guest post

By doing this I could see exactly what activities went on in each segment of the business. Then, inside each activity I wrote out all of the information that related to it:

- When the activity needed to take place.

- What steps were involved in completing the activity.

- Who, if anyone, was helping to complete it.

So for example, here's what I wrote out for my Tuesday Video post:

Make video:

- Prepare topic – Carrie

- Write script – Carrie

- Set up filming and film – Carrie and James/or Emily

- Edit video – Emily or Carrie

- Upload to YouTube – James

Write content for post it will be shared with:

- Title/headline – James

- Compelling intro – James/Carrie

- Overview of what viewer will learn from the video – James

- Call to action to get them to leave a comment (ask viewer a question to answer in the comments) – James

- YouTube subscribe button – James

- Embed YouTube video – James

- Click to Tweet under the video, so people can share post via Twitter easily – James

- Include freebie, if there is one (write text, create graphic, create sign-up box via LeadPages so people can sign up) – Jess and Michelle

- Share info about guest expert, if there is one – James

- Write out breakdown of the top tips shared in the video – James

- Summary – James

- Create call to action to get people to comment – James

- Add subscription box, so people don't miss next week's video – James

- Carrie to check over everything

Create graphics for the post:

- Featured image for post – Michelle

- Image to go at the top of the post – Michelle

- Images to use on social media – Michelle

Marketing the post:

- Share via weekly email to entire audience – Carrie

- Share via Facebook Ads – Carrie

- Share via social media multiple times throughout the week and in the future – Michelle

- If there's an expert in the video, email a link and ask if they'd like to share it with their audience – James

This is a snapshot of the entire process of what it takes to put together my Tuesday post. Having it mapped out like this gives me a broader view, so I know exactly what needs to happen and who's taking care of each task. Within each task, I've drilled down even more to write out extra steps, processes, and guidelines to help make sure everything stays consistent.

Doing this has not only made me far more organized, but it means that as I expand the team, my systems are already in place to make it easier to show new team members exactly what they need to do.

Don't get me wrong, I still have plenty of moments of feeling ridiculously overwhelmed, but the difference now is that I have a toolbox of secret weapons that help me to pull (sometimes heave) myself back on track and get to grips with everything.

Building a successful business requires so much focus, yet when you're in the midst of building it, it's so easy to feel like a headless chicken, going around in circles. You have so much to do, and everything feels like such a mess that you don't even know where to begin, but you have to force yourself to get a grip. You have to take back control, refocus, and keep moving forward.

While we all accomplish this in different ways, creating a business timetable and having a business hub has helped me so much.

SHE TAKES ACTION

To create your business hub, you'll need to start by creating a business map – so you can see exactly how all of the elements fit together. Your business map could be a list or a chart – whatever works best for you.

An example is shown opposite.

Identify all of your business activities and then drill down into each one and map out what steps you have to take in order to complete it and when you have to take them.

There's a lot going on in the example opposite. Yours might look way simpler. In fact, hopefully it does, otherwise you're going to be spinning far too many plates!

I've got a free template, worksheet and video to help you with this, which you can download at http://bit.ly/SMB-Resources

YOU, THE CEO				

MARKETING	SALES	CLIENT MANAGEMENT	ADMIN	FINANCIAL
Blogging	Consulting	Client scheduling	RESEARCH	Tracking expenses
Direct outreach	(evergreen) programs	Privacy policy	Blogs to follow	Bill payment
Keep in touch	Physical product	Contests	Shareables	Managing bank accounts
Freebies	Group coaching	Testimonials	Guest blogging	Tax returns
Videos	1-on-1 coaching	Surveys	Events to attend	Bookkeeping
Newsletters		Questionnaires	Experts to interview	Reimbursements
Webinars		Delivery structures	Be interviewed by	Payment collection
Contents		Client support	WEBSITE	Client invoicing
Interviews		Client intake	Upload/format posts	
Email marketing			Maintenance – updates	
Case studies			Maintenance – backups	
PARTNERSHIPS			Maintenance – installations	
Joint ventures			SEO	
Affiliates			Google analytics	
Referrals			misc. tasks	
SOCIAL MEDIA			Quarterly business reviews	
Instagram			Updating calendar	
Pinterest			Email processing	
Google +				
Facebook				
Twitter				

207

GROWING A TEAM AND
FINDING A MENTOR

For the first few years of building FEA, I would often daydream about having a team of people to help me, because at times I felt so stressed out doing it largely by myself. In fact, I wrote the following entry in my journal, which sums up perfectly how I often felt:

> *'I feel like I'm doing absolutely everything myself – I'm trying to be good at everything, when really I'm not good. I'm fumbling my way through. I wish I had a team of people to do things I'm not good at.'*
> **MY JOURNAL, JANUARY 9, 2012**

The reality was, I couldn't afford to pay people, and things were so jumbled, I'm not sure what I could have got anyone to do.

Looking back now, I'm so grateful I didn't have the money to bring anyone on board, because it forced me to get good. It forced me to figure things out, even if I was fumbling my way through most of the time.

I learned so much and I grew. And the more I grew, the better my ideas and decisions became. I'm not sure I'd be where I am today if I hadn't had to push myself to grow so much at the beginning.

There were times (and still are times) when my head would feel like it was going to explode because I was trying to learn so much! But the satisfaction of figuring something out far outweighed the struggle.

If you're still the only person in your business, embrace it. Use it as a way to stretch yourself and to grow. It will help you to blossom into an incredible entrepreneur.

Growing a team, one person at a time

There comes a time, though, when you need to expand and get help, and that time for me came a year into working on FEA. When I started working on my magazine idea, I knew I had to hire someone who had experience designing magazines. And as soon as I made the decision, Natalie Walstein came into my life.

I reached out to her, told her my idea, we signed the contract (very important), and she became the first FEA team member.

It was just the two of us for a while, and then as things developed I realized I needed more help if I was going to focus on growing FEA.

Through a recommendation, I hired someone to help me with social media and blog posts. We had a trial period of three months, and during that time I realized that even though she was great, she wasn't the right fit for FEA. We had a completely different vibe, and as she was creating content for FEA, it just felt off brand. It was a good lesson to learn – only hire people who resonate with you and truly understand your brand.

A few months later, I ended up bringing on board the amazing Michelle Rohr whose stories I've been sharing throughout this book. She was a massive fan of FEA and had reached out to me and told me how much she loved it. She said she would love to help in any way she could. She'd already contributed a few articles to the magazine, and I'd loved them, so I felt like she would be the perfect fit.

She started by helping me out with my social media – creating graphics, posting out, and helping me with blog posts. Within a week, I realized how incredible she was. She quickly took social media off my plate and did such an amazing job that I no longer had to worry about it. I felt like a weight had been lifted, and I finally had more time to get on with developing my ideas for FEA.

As FEA grew, I brought more people on board. I started with a web developer, who I found through ThemeForest.net. I liked one of the Wordpress themes on there, so reached out to the developers to see if they could customize it for me. I started to work with Andrei, who I've been working with ever since. After spending years trying to figure out how to build websites myself, finally having a developer was like the dreamiest thing ever! For the first time, I was able to create a website that felt and looked exactly how I wanted it to.

When I launched the Members' Club, running FEA became chaotic. There was so much to do, so much to keep up with, and so much to develop, at times I felt like the business was swallowing me whole.

Looking back now, I have no idea how I managed to keep growing it all and stay sane. But I did, because I had to. It was part of the deal I made with myself when I decided to become unstoppable.

There were definitely elements of my business that suffered. I barely had any time to market the membership site properly, because I could barely keep up with creating the content for it! But there's something I believe in:

We're all in the right place at the right time.

I think that if I'd had someone on board to help me with marketing, it wouldn't have been as effective because I wasn't in the right place. In fact, I did actually bring someone on board, tentatively and for a very short time, to help with marketing. It didn't work out at all because I wasn't in the right place, and FEA wasn't in the right place to be marketed aggressively – I wouldn't have been able to cope.

The next person to join the FEA team was Jessica Thenhaus. She came on board to help clear my plate. I found her through a recommendation in my Facebook group, checked out her website, liked what I saw, and arranged to have a call.

As it happened, she was already a member of FEA, so she knew all about it (bonus). We hit it off and started a trial. Within weeks, I knew it was a perfect fit. She dealt with all the support emails and made my life so much easier.

Then came the next step, hiring a mentor.

Finding someone a few steps ahead

I knew I'd done a pretty darn good job to build a membership of over 1,400 people within a year, all by myself, with no clue or experience. I was proud of myself, but I also knew that to get to the next level, I had to learn from someone who was ahead of me, someone who had built a bigger membership site than me.

The only person I could think of was Michael Hyatt. His membership site was much bigger than mine, so I thought he might be able to help. I finally had the money coming in and was in a place where I could implement the strategies. So, I reached out and asked if he was available for one-to-one mentoring. Turns out he was fully booked! I was devastated.

Luckily, the universe worked its magic – as she always does when you get intentional – and after I told a friend that Michael was fully booked, she suggested Stu McLaren, Michael's strategic business partner for Platform University. Stu had loads of experience building membership sites, had just sold out of his other business and was looking to start doing more one-on-one coaching.

It was like music to my ears! I got so excited, and as soon as I got off the call I Googled his name, found his website, and emailed him.

A few days went by, and I hadn't heard back, so in my excitement I emailed again. Weeks went by, and I began to panic because I knew I had to work with him, so I emailed again and again. I honestly felt like such a nuisance, but I knew I had to keep trying.

Eventually, an email showed up in my inbox from Stu, and I was over the moon! He was available for coaching, and he'd just been busy doing a big launch, which is why it took him so long to get back to me.

After an initial call, I knew working with him would be the best thing. I stumped up $7,500 and traveled all the way from the UK to Canada for a one-day coaching session with him. It was the largest amount of money I'd ever spent on one thing for FEA, but it felt right.

I arrived for our meeting the next morning at 8:30 a.m. in the Orchid Boardroom, and shortly after, Stu arrived. He started by saying how great what I'd created was and that he really believed in FEA. For the first time since starting FEA, I realized how important it is to have people who you look up to believe in you. Stu believed in me and that made me feel like anything was possible.

We spent the day chatting about how I was going to grow my membership site and creating a plan of action for what I needed to do. I came away feeling so positive and fired up about everything. Sometimes, all it takes to have a breakthrough is to work with the right people who can help you to up-level, people who are a few steps ahead of where you're at now and who can help show you the way.

When I got back from Canada, I knew I had my work cut out for me. The plan was to change the membership site from being open for enrollment all the time to being open for enrollment twice a year, for seven days each time. Stu told me this model worked really well because it was easier to do a big welcome for everyone joining at the same time, it created scarcity, and forced people to make a decision as to whether or not they wanted to join. It would also mean that for 90 percent of the year, I was able to focus on just making the Members' Club amazing, not worrying about marketing it.

So, I set myself a goal to do a launch in June and to get 1,200 new members on board.

Working with Stu forced me to up my game. He told me to test out launching with a three-part video series, a free workbook, and a live webinar, in the lead-up to the enrollment of the Members' Club.

I'd never done a big launch like it before, but knew if I wanted to breakthrough, I had to put myself out there like never before.

He helped me to write the scripts for my video series and craft the emails for my launch campaign and he encouraged me every step of the way.

I ended the launch on 1,240 new members, and the feedback was amazing. It blew my mind to think that I had more members join in seven days than joined in the first year! It was a huge breakthrough, and it was because I'd worked so hard to get myself in the right position to work with someone like Stu, implement the strategies, and reap the rewards.

As the year drew to a close, I did my final enrollment for the year with my goal in mind – to close out the year on 3,000 members. We closed on 3,091. The power of intention is incredible, I'm telling you.

Growing the FEA team and finding a mentor has been crucial to the growth of FEA. I would never have been able to have the breakthroughs without them, but bringing them on board happened over time. I had to get myself and FEA to a place where I was actually in the position to utilize the help on hand.

SHE TAKES ACTION

You really do have to surround yourself with amazing people who are there to support your growth; when you do you will flourish.

Just make sure you:

- *Find the right people to bring on board. Make sure you like them, make sure they resonate with you and your brand, and have a call before hiring them, or meet up if you can.*

- *Set up a trial period to work with them, maybe 30 days or three months, to see how you get on.*

- *Make sure you sign contracts, which outline exactly what they're going to be doing and what you're going to be paying them.*

- *Have realistic expectations. It's too easy to hire someone and think they're going to have a magic wand and fix all of your issues. This is never going to happen. But people can help to fix the issues and make your business run more smoothly, just don't expect the world from someone. Also, allow people to grow, develop, and get into their stride.*

- *If it doesn't work out with someone, be honest about it. Let that person know that they are not the right fit for you. It's better for both of you to be honest.*

GATHER YOUR
BUSINESS
FRIENDS

It had been a few weeks since I'd finished the first big launch for the Members' Club, and I was in a funk. While the launch had gone amazingly well, I felt an overwhelming urge to hibernate. I felt detached from FEA, my motivation had disappeared, and I began to panic, 'What's going on? Why do I feel like this?' I started to overanalyze everything and quickly realized I needed to do something about it.

It was time for a chat with Nikki Elledge Brown, who, as I write this, I've never actually met in real life. She lives over 7,000 miles away in Hawaii but thanks to the Internet she came into my life, and has made it all the more magnificent.

I went to my laptop and called her on FaceTime. We spent the next hour chatting about business and life. I told her my panic about not being motivated and feeling disconnected from FEA after my launch. She told me she experienced the same thing after her launch.

Ah, relief. It was OK for me to feel that way; I was just human and it was OK to go through a lull sometimes.

By the end of the call, I felt so much better about everything. She'd given me a pep talk to fire me back up, and I felt inspired again.

That's what business friends do. They're there for you when you need them (and vice versa, of course), to lift you up, to tell you it's OK, to share their experiences with you, to just be on your journey with you, and to give you a kick up the backside when you need it!

My friend Jason did this for me back in June 2011. When I was freaking out about launching the first issue of my magazine, I told him how I was feeling and expected him to sympathize with me, but he did the complete opposite! He gave me a huge kick up the backside and told me to 'stick to my original plan,' which meant launching in three days' time.

When he said those words to me, my instincts told me he was right. I knew I'd been taken over by fear and what I had to do was step up and get my magazine out there. With his words ringing in my ears, I made the decision to launch.

If we hadn't had that conversation, I'm pretty sure I would have convinced myself to push back the launch by a few months.

It's amazing what impact your business friends can have.

Building a business can be so unbelievably lonely. We don't have colleagues to hang out with and chat to about the things we're going through, so we need to create them through friendships with people who truly get it.

Nikki calls her business friends her 'Cabinet of Friendtors,' which I love. We all need a Cabinet of Friendtors.

I honestly think I'd go insane without mine. They help restore my belief in myself when I lose it, they encourage me to play big and to achieve amazing things, they help to make me unstoppable.

SHE TAKES ACTION

Who could you invite to join your Cabinet of Friendtors? Make a list, reach out to them for a chat, and start building beautiful friendships.

LISTEN TO YOURSELF

Aside from your business friends, there's someone else whose friendship you really need in order to be unstoppable, and that's your own.

You need to build a deep relationship with yourself so that you learn to listen to yourself and trust yourself completely.

While the opinions and advice of others might be very helpful at times, this is your life and your business, and you're the one steering your ship so you have to be in charge. You can't rely on other people to show you the route you need to take. You have to trust yourself and your instincts and listen closely to them, so you make the best decisions for you.

I've found an amazing way to connect with myself is to journal. When I allow my thoughts to tumble onto the pages, I connect more with what's going on in my life, the way I'm feeling, and the decisions I'm making. Journaling gives me the quiet time I need to tune in with myself and that's what we need to do in order to make the best decisions.

I'll often start by thinking about my day or thinking about a challenge or experience I'm having, and I'll begin to write about it and allow whatever comes up to come up. I find that when I do this I go deeper and deeper within and realize things I never consciously acknowledged before. Sometimes, words end up on the page, and I have no idea where they came from, but they appeared there, giving me amazing guidance. I've learned to trust it, to trust what comes up.

When I'm struggling to make a decision and don't know what the best thing to do is, I'll have a conversation out loud with myself, often when I'm driving alone. I'll just start talking about the decision I need to make and allow myself to talk. Sometimes a load of nonsense comes out, but then usually I'll dig so deep within myself, I'll hear my intuition speak up, and I know what I need to do.

Another thing I often do that helps me is I close my eyes and go to meet FEA. In my mind, she's this big glow of purple-white light. She doesn't have a face or a form, really, but it's her, and I just walk over and hug her. I feel this immense amount of love I have for her and an incredible amount of gratitude that together we're building a wonderful business around our mission. I remind myself of what the mission is and I have a conversation with her about what's going on in the business and I ask her my business questions and see what she thinks. It's kind of like a 'What would Richard Branson do?' type thing. Sometimes it takes me a while to shut off my logical brain and allow the conversation to really get underway; you just have to stick with it, have fun and allow whatever wants to come out, to come out.

This might sound REALLY crazy, but you have to do whatever it takes to keep figuring things out and keep moving forward.

I realize that this advice would never be given at business school, but we're not in business school right now and this is all about you taking a dream that's inside your head and turning it into reality. That, in itself, is pretty magical, so get creative and use your imagination to help you see the path ahead.

Following your dreams and turning your ideas into reality is a lonely path. No one else can do it for you, so you have to be tuned in with yourself, you have to pay attention to your intuition, it's talking to you all the time; just take action to turn up the volume, listen and watch for the signs.

DON'T CARRY YOUR MISTAKES AROUND WITH YOU

Since starting my first business in 2005, I have made a lot of mistakes. Some were really small, and some were really big. I've lost money. I've messed up websites. I've got things wrong with customers. I've had tough times with business partners. These weren't easy times to get through, but I kept going. The best part is that I learned so much by making those mistakes. I grew wiser, I grew stronger, and I became better.

It's easy to become scared and ashamed of your mistakes, but I'm proud of mine. They have helped me to become the entrepreneur I am today. I'm not perfect, far from it, but I've learned how to bounce back, I've learned how to handle mistakes and setbacks, and I've learned how to be better, and for that I'm so grateful.

Don't let your mistakes get you down or make you think you're not good enough. Instead, change your perspective and place them under your feet and use them to grow.

Dan Millman puts it well in his book, *Body Mind Mastery: Creating Success in Sports and Life*:

> *'If babies held the same tendency toward self-criticism as adults, they might never learn to walk or talk. Can you imagine infants stomping, 'Aarggh! Screwed up again!'*

Sometimes you mess up, and that's OK. Do yourself a massive favor and be gentle with yourself. You wouldn't be so harsh with a child when it made a mistake or criticize a colleague or a friend that way, so don't do it to yourself!

When you make the wrong call, or people get annoyed and unsubscribe, or people email you to let you know that you did something wrong, it's often followed by a sinking feeling. You wish you could turn back time, think things through better, and make a different decision, but you can't.

Even though I don't like making mistakes and annoying people, looking back, I'm actually glad I did make those mistakes, because I learned something from each one. I learned not to make the same mistake again.

Sometimes, you have to go wrong in order to learn how to go right. And it's all OK. It's part of the adventure.

CELEBRATE THE WINS

I find that we entrepreneurs are so goal-oriented that often we achieve something and straight away we're onto the next goal and we never even stop to take it all in and celebrate. But the simple act of celebrating can help us to become unstoppable, because it makes us take a step back and recognize the progress we're actually making.

So, if you get a new customer, celebrate. If you reach a subscriber/fan/follower goal, celebrate. If you learn a new lesson, celebrate. If a customer says something amazing about you or your business, celebrate (in fact, store these in a folder called 'Amazing feedback' and read when feeling down and it'll instantly make you feel good about things!).

Celebrate your wins, big, small or tiny and feel good about them. Crack out the champagne, do a happy dance, share your success with someone else.

Be proud of yourself.

SHE TAKES ACTION

What have you achieved lately, which you didn't stop to properly acknowledge or celebrate? Celebrate it now! Woohoo :-)

Enjoy the journey & celebrate the wins.

TAKE CARE OF YOURSELF

As well as making the time to celebrate your wins, you also have to make time for self-care. This is something I have struggled with a lot. I get so excited and so obsessed with my goals and with growing my business, I forget to take care of myself. I just want to work and work and work to achieve something, with no regard for what impact it's having on me, because I LOVE to be in the flow of work. However, in the past, this has led to me feeling burned-out, which then leads to me being very unproductive!

I will be honest though, there are times when I need to work like a maniac, because I want to make massive progress and sometimes that requires me to work on another level. Balance is something that I've struggled with and in my opinion, I'm not even sure it really exists. However, there are things we can all do to ensure we look after ourselves, so we don't derail.

I make time to exercise – it gets me out of my head and into my body, whether it's a walk in the park or a personal training session (which I now do multiple times a week).

I make time to have fun and love to spend time with my dogs, enjoy a glass of wine, or just chill out with my friends and family. I make time to have a Reiki session every now and again to just relax. I also have coaching sessions, where I get to talk all about how I'm feeling and what's going on. I now make time to get away and (try to) switch off – this is something I never did at the beginning, but now I make a conscious effort to plan trips away throughout the year to give myself some downtime.

SHE TAKES ACTION

What could you do to take more care of yourself? Think about it, write it down and make sure that you make time for it.

RESIST THE URGE TO KEEP
PUTTING THINGS OFF

There have been so many times when I've wanted to put off doing what I knew I needed to do. It took three years to actually turn my idea to create a platform for women into reality. It took me four years to finally write this book. It took me a year to finally create my membership site. I nearly put off launching my magazine.

It happens to all of us – we make up excuses as to why we're not quite ready and need to wait.

Get honest with yourself about what these things are, accept them, and then let them go. Do not allow them to stop you.

Sure, they might hold you back for a while, as I've experienced, but don't let them stop you. It's never too late to begin.

WHEN IT ALL FEELS
IMPOSSIBLE...

*'In those moments when you feel like hope is gone and like you're
crazy, remember that life is for doing crazy things and for taking risks.
So don't be scared. Be the superhero inside of yourself – be bold, have
courage and always believe. Re-read when feeling down or lost!'*
MY JOURNAL, OCTOBER 13, 2011

While giving myself that pep talk, I was sitting in a hotel room, after a
three-day course about product creation. It was the first time I'd stayed
away by myself for business, and in the quietness of the room, I began to
think about what I was doing.

The weeks leading up to the course had been tough. I'd met with various
people and told them what I was working on and none of them got it.
They looked at me like I had no business sense at all. They made me feel
small. Correction, I allowed them to let me feel small.

I was vulnerable. I was at the beginning of my journey with FEA, I had
hardly anything figured out, and most of the time it all felt impossible. I
felt like I was at the bottom of a huge mountain, and I wasn't sure I could
make it, but I knew deep down that I definitely had the stamina to try,
which is why I wrote myself a pep talk.

When you're feeling down, when things feel impossible, when hope eludes you, when you've lost all of your motivation and you feel like you're drifting, give yourself a pep talk. Remind yourself of who you need to be, lift yourself up, give yourself permission to proceed.

Once you've had a pep talk, set yourself a challenge to turn things around!

This is one of my favorite things to do (and I've had to do it a lot over the years, because I'm always falling off the entrepreneurial bandwagon!).

It actually happened to me recently. I'd just got married and I was spending the summer in California with my husband. I'd planned to take some time off to enjoy being a newlywed, but as the weeks and months rolled by I struggled to get my work mojo back.

I literally couldn't be bothered to do any work. I felt unmotivated, uninspired, and lost. *Urgh!*

After a while of feeling like this I snapped, I'd had enough and I knew I needed to pull myself up and get back on track.

So I took myself off to a lake with a notepad and pen, and spent some time reconnecting with my business dreams and goals (because I'd completely disconnected from them).

I just sat there quietly and allowed myself to dream. I then scribbled everything out and finally my dreams and goals were no longer a jumbled mess in my head that I couldn't decipher, they were finally on paper for me to see. I instantly felt better.

After my dreaming brain dump had ended, the next thing I did was concoct a daily routine for myself. I wrote out simple actions I could take every day to help me get out of my funk and back into the flow of business.

On my list were things from my Mission: Success Challenge.

- Take time to visualize and connect with a goal.

- Set aside time for personal development (reading a book, watching an inspiring video, listening to a podcast).

- Create daily goals and game plan, so I'm focused.

- Check in with myself throughout the day – set a timer on my phone to remind myself to think about what I'm doing, where my thoughts are and if I'm on track.

- Exercise – I needed to stop just sitting in front on my laptop and get my body moving.

- Have fun – yep, I put this on my daily activity list to help me get my mojo back and just feel good every day.

- Have quiet time to meditate, relax and tune in with myself.

- Think of what I'm grateful for each night.

I made it my mission to do those things every single day for 30 days straight. I even created a cute printable for myself and ticked off each activity every day to help me stay on track.

By the end of the first day I was a new person. By the second I was on fire. I was ridiculously productive, coming up with new ideas and getting so much done.

I felt back in the flow and inspired. Entrepreneurial bliss.

I called it my 30-day Miracle Month challenge. What a miracle it was.

SHE TAKES ACTION

The next time you're in a funk or drifting aimlessly, do the Miracle Month Challenge for yourself (you can download it at http://bit.ly/ SMB-Resources) and turn things around.

You might also like to commit the following affirmation to paper and repeat it to yourself daily, or whenever you need a boost.

'I am brave, courageous and I can do this. All that I need flows to me in miraculous ways.'

It's amazing what an impact it has when we make the decision to uplift ourselves.

'When the world says, "Give up," Hope whispers, "Try it one more time."'

Unknown

YOU ARE HERE

*'I think I am a bit mad for pursuing FEA, but we are born and then
we die and it's up to us to make the bit in between amazing,'*
MY JOURNAL, DECEMBER 25, 2011

One of the things that has helped me to become unstoppable in the pursuit of my business dreams – and my dreams, in general – is the thought that we live on this planet we call Earth, which hovers in blackness, surrounded by stars, and other planets we don't really know much about. Then, further out into the blackness, there is an entire universe that we can't even comprehend. Yet somehow, here we are.

**We are all special. We are all worthy. We are all capable
of greatness. We are all equal, because we are all here.**

I'm not about to waste my opportunity here, are you?

In the moments leading up to a TEDx Talk I did back in 2014 in front of nearly 1,000 people, all I kept thinking was, 'I'm on a planet that hovers in blackness, in a universe so huge it blows my mind. It doesn't matter if I mess up! In this huge, crazy universe, somehow I'm here, and I'm going to go out there and give it my all.'

Thinking about what's out there in the blackness of our universe makes me realize how significant and insignificant life is all at the same time. It doesn't matter if we mess up a million times. What matters is that we strive to create and do the things we want to do. What matters is that we follow our hearts. What matters is that we use our gifts. What matters is that we live meaningful, happy lives.

Because otherwise, what is the point?

We have to have the courage to dream big and to go for it – that's how you become a successful entrepreneur, and every single one of us can do it.

IT ALL SLOTS INTO PLACE EVENTUALLY

'I feel like FEA and all of my thoughts over the past few years are finally slotting into place. I'm starting to realize that I have to move forward without fear of something unconventional, but with faith that it will work out for the best. If I give up my dream I'm giving it up for money, security and to fit into society. If I persevere and succeed I can show others what is possible.'

MY JOURNAL, DECEMBER 25, 2011

After writing that journal entry, it took me another four years to really get things where I wanted them to be, but that first year for me was the most important. It was the year that I worked on figuring out what on earth I was doing. It was the year I decided to condition myself for success and just go for my dreams. It was the year that forced me to get in tune with myself, trust myself, and trust my ideas. It was the year that helped me to feel like things were finally slotting into place.

That year cemented my commitment to building the Female Entrepreneur Association, even though I'd made less than $1,000 from working so hard at it. Some people might have thought that by the end of my first year FEA was a complete failure, because it wasn't generating any revenue, but I'd learned to listen to my instincts, and they were telling me, 'Keep going, you're on the right path.'

Maybe to the ordinary person I was barking mad, but that's what we have to be as entrepreneurs. We have to be barking mad about our ideas and our dreams in order to pursue them with zero guarantee that they'll work out.

It makes for a fun, exhilarating, and somewhat scary adventure.

Year two was full of learning, growing, and understanding how to create something of value for my audience. I chose to pursue the magazine idea. I learned all about growing my network, I networked online and offline like a crazy person, won an award, hit a financial roadblock, and realized how much I needed to adjust my mindset on money. There were so many moments of joy and utter despair in year two, but I kept on going.

Year three was all about growing my network and figuring out how to make it financially sustainable. I was determined not to end the year without figuring out how I could make it work. I fought with myself so much, and fear got in the way a lot, but I pushed through. Finally, on November 26, 2013, I launched the Members' Club.

Year four was all about figuring out how to make the Members' Club a success. I experimented, explored ideas, and had to work out how to manage it all. I set an ambitious goal to have 1,000 members by the end of the year, and I hit it. I finally figured out how to reach a goal by a deadline!

Year five was all about scaling my success. I expanded my team, hired a mentor, and changed the way I was running my business. It tripled in size, and I finally reached my goal of hitting over $84,000 in revenue a month. My mind was blown.

Year six is where I am now, which has been all about stepping up even more by writing this book and up-leveling my business by expanding the team even more and growing.

It has been an amazing adventure and I've still got so much more learning, growing and exploring to do, but the big lesson I've learned is something Mahatma Gandhi said very well:

'The future depends on what you do today.'

What are you going to do today to make sure that you move in the direction of your dreams, turn your ideas into reality, and build a wildly successful business?

The world is changing, more and more people are waking up to the realization that there's more for them to be doing. More and more people are answering their inner knowing that is whispering, 'There's more for you.'

You are being called to show up for your dreams, to step up and shine like never before, to create the life you're meant to live.

So, answer back.

Explore your entrepreneurial path, and see where it takes you. Condition yourself for success to help you along the way and become unstoppable in the pursuit of it all.

You can make the most magnificent things happen when you allow yourself to just go for it.

So say to yourself, 'I can and I will. Watch me.'

· THE CHECKLIST ·

She's Unstoppable

Here's a reminder of what you need to do in order to become unstoppable in the pursuit of building a wildly successful business.

O   Honor the process of being an entrepreneur – the ups and the downs.

O   Keep the faith and trust that everything will work out.

O   Be ridiculously persistent in the pursuit of your dreams.

O   Practice makes perfect, so practice getting good at becoming a wildly successful entrepreneur.

O   Take control of your business by creating a business hub, systemizing your processes and creating a business timetable for yourself.

O   Listen to yourself and allow the answers to unfold.

O   Use your mistakes as a stepping-stone for growing.

O   Surround yourself with people who believe in you and can help show you the way.

O   Be really consistent in taking action that will get you closer to your dreams.

O   Take care of yourself, as well as your business; you are precious.

O   Remember that you can 100 percent do this. The world is ready and waiting for you to shine.

I can & I will. Watch me.

THANK YOU

We've come to the end of our journey together in this book and I'd like to thank you for reading it. Getting this book out of my head and onto paper has been one of the most challenging things I've ever done, it's pushed me so far out of my comfort zone. I resisted it for such a long time, but eventually I gave in and chose to just go for it.

Turning our ideas into reality isn't always easy, everyone struggles with it to some degree, but it's well worth it, and my hope is that the blueprint you'll find on the next page will help you to put everything that I've shared in the book into action.

Remember that you can achieve the most incredible things, so commit to it.

You're wonderful and amazing and I wish you so much success along your beautiful journey.

With so much love,

Carrie xx

P.S. Don't forget to visit http://bit.ly/SMB-Resources and download all the goodies that accompany this book

And let's keep on hanging out together – you can find me here:

Facebook:
www.facebook.com/FemaleEntrepreneurAssociation

YouTube:
www.youtube.com/FemaleEntrepreneur

Instagram:
@iamcarriegreen

Snapchat:
@carriegreen_fea

Twitter:
@iamcarriegreen

THE 28-DAY
SHE MEANS BUSINESS
CHALLENGE

The 28-Day She Means Business Challenge draws together all the actions of the book and I hope you find it a helpful guide on your journey to getting your ideas out into the world.

Week 1: The exploration begins...

Day 1: Get yourself a brand new journal

Write on the first page, 'My entrepreneurial adventure: Mission Success.' And underneath write the date.

On the next page write your first entry, stating where you're at in your life right now and what your dreams are. Write down that you're committing to a mission to create more success in your life, to show up for your dreams more than ever before, and to step up and get your ideas out into the world in a bigger way. Also, write down why you're making this commitment to yourself and what you want to achieve by committing to it.

From this day forward try to write in your journal once a day, updating it with the experiences you're having along your journey.

See also page 19.

Day 2: Create your vision board

Today start collecting inspiration, tear-out quotes, get dreaming, and create your vision board. To help you with this watch the video about it on the She Means Business resource page. There's also a free printable with lots of inspirational quotes on http://bit.ly/SMB-Resources

Once you've created your board put it somewhere you'll see it every day and over the next few weeks take time to go and stand in front of your board and connect with everything on it.

See also page 22.

Day 3: Visualize

Start to visualize what you want on a daily basis from now on. Either close your eyes and follow along with the 12-step process on page 47, or go to http://bit.ly/SMB-Resources and download the free, guided visualization I've created and listen to it daily

See also page 42.

Day 4: Create inspirational playlists – music and videos

Put together a list of inspiring music to listen to and a list of inspiring videos to watch. This will ensure you always have some mojo at your fingertips!

See also page 62.

Day 5: Pay attention to your posture

Throughout the day pay attention to your posture. Stand or sit tall, shoulders back and relaxed. Really tune in with your body and align it so that you feel relaxed and confident.

See also page 59.

Day 6: Watch your thoughts

Get a piece of paper and every hour take a moment to write down what thoughts you've been thinking over the past hour and how you've been feeling (if need be, set a reminder to go off every hour on your phone). This exercise will force you to tune in more with your thoughts.

The aim here is to move away from the negative thoughts that are holding you back and to start focusing more on positive thoughts that will spur you forward. Keep this up and start proactively checking in with what's going on in your mind, it's so transformational.

See also page 53.

Day 7: Review

Take a moment to write down three or more things that you're most grateful for and then spend some time thinking about those things and really feel the gratitude from within.

Take some time to write down your big wins and realizations over the past week. Have you had any 'aha' moments? If so, write them down. Has anything come up that you've realized you need to work on? If so, write it down.

Take a deep breath and get excited about the coming week.

Week 2: Getting clarity

Day 8: Goals and intentions

This week is all about getting clarity, so start today by setting your goals and intentions for the future – for today, for this week and month, and for the next six months or year. In fact, feel free to dream as far into the future as you want. Do whatever feels right for you. Have fun with this and release any limitations. Once you've thought about what you want, write it down.

As a side project consider creating a goal board or a goal box or a goal folder for yourself. It's so much fun and so powerful.

See also page 46.

Day 9: Mission statement

Take some time today to write out your mission statement. Write one for your personal life – what's your personal mission in life?

Then write out your business mission statement – what do you want to achieve for your business?

My mission is to help inspire and empower as many women as possible from around the world to build successful businesses.

This is my complete business focus. What's yours? Write it down.

See also page 92.

Day 10: Game plan

So now you have clarity around your business goals and vision, let's make a game plan!

Today think about your big vision and then break it down and write out what you'll need to do in order to make it happen.

- What do you need to learn?

- Who can help you?

- What resources or websites could help you?

- What actions will you need to take?

- Plot out when you need to take these actions. Assign a completion date to each action item.

See also page 165.

Day 11: Brand values

Get even more connected to your business today by thinking about what your brand values are. What is at the heart and soul of your business? Write down five words that describe your values.

See also page 97.

Day 12: Who are your audience?

Take some time today to really think about your audience and tune in with them. Who are they? What do they love? What are their desires? What are their frustrations and challenges (internal and external), how can you help them?

Consider starting a Pinterest board to pin anything that represents your audience. You can come back to it time and time again to reconnect with them.

See also page 98.

Day 13: How will you wow?

Today is all about upping the ante on how you wow and delight your audience. First, write down what you're doing at the moment to go above and beyond to delight your audience. Review what you've written and then brainstorm new ways you could go above and beyond to wow them.

Break down every step of your customer journey, starting with all of the potential ways they could discover you (social media, Google, referral, ads, etc.) to the ways you stay in touch with them and build a relationship with them, then think about how they become a customer and what happens once they are a customer.

At each of these touch points, think of what else you could do to improve the customer experience.

See also page 107.

Day 14: Review

We're at the end of the second week, so take some time to write down what's happened over the past week. Write down any lessons learned, any 'aha' moments.

Once you've done that think of three or more things you're grateful for, write them down and then spend some time thinking about them and feeling the gratitude.

Week 3: Leverage the Internet

Day 15: Choose your focus

This week is all about you leveraging the Internet to build a successful business. So today I want you to think about and write down your core marketing strategy for growing your business, using the Internet.

See also page 112.

Day 16: Set your goals

Today think about and write down your goal for growth. How do you want to grow over the next few months? Get clear about it. Set a deadline and commit to your growth. If you don't know how you want to grow, chances are you won't grow, so get super clear.

See also page 165.

Day 17: Find out where your audience is

Take some time to go over where your audience hangs out online. What Facebook groups are they in? What social media platform do they use the most? Where can you find them? Just brainstorm and write it all down.

See also page 147.

Day 18: Ask what they want, communicate with them

Today reach out to your audience, chat with them, ask them what their biggest frustrations are or ask them what they'd most love help with or ask them a question that will help you to get to know them better. Communication is the key.

See also page 114.

Day 19: Get yourself out there

Today focus on taking action to get yourself and your business out there. What one thing could you do today that is big (and maybe scares you!) that would help to get your business more visibility? Do it. Take massive action today!!

See also page 125.

Day 20: Release money blocks

Today focus on allowing money to flow to you by downloading the money visualization I've created at http://bit.ly/SMB-Resources. Listen to it daily to help you to get into the mindset of allowing money to flow freely to you.

See also page 151.

Day 21: Review

Today is the end of week three! Take some time to review the past week – what's happened? What did you achieve? What did you learn? What do you need to improve? Did you have any 'aha' moments? Write it all down.

Now, think of three or more things you're grateful for, write them down and then spend some time really feeling the gratitude you have for them.

Week 4: Connections

Day 22: Create your friendtors

This week is all about making connections and expanding your support network. So today, make a list of all your business friends and people who support you along your journey. Reach out to as many of these people as you can today and let them know how much you appreciate them.

Next, make a list of people who you'd love to reach out to and build a great friendship with. Message at least one of these people today and start a conversation :-) you never know where it might lead.

See also page 215.

Day 23: Who can help you?

Now you've got your list of business friends down, have a think about any mentors who could help you. Are there any areas of your business where you'd like to work with someone that's a few steps ahead of you to help you grow? You might not know of specific people yet, but just get clear on what areas of business you'd like help with – the right people will begin to show up when you get intentional.

I've loved working with mentors over my journey. I work with someone to help me move past my internal blocks and I also work with someone to help me accelerate my business growth. Both are incredibly valuable to me.

See also page 208.

Day 24: Websites and podcasts

While working with people can be so transformational, you can learn a lot from working with people indirectly through websites, podcasts, and videos. So today make a list of the websites, podcasts, videos, and brands that can help you throughout your entrepreneurial journey.

I've compiled a list of people who you might love here at http://bit.ly/SMB-Resources

See also page 61.

Day 25: What groups could you join?

If you don't want to work one-on-one with people, but want more help than a website can offer, you might want to consider joining specific groups or memberships.

So today, go on Facebook and look to see if there are any relevant groups you could join. Are there any online programs you'd like to enroll in? Any membership groups you'd love to join?

If you want to be part of my membership site, I'd love to have you on board. You can find out more at http://bit.ly/SMB-Resources

See also page 28.

Day 26: Offline networking

Today write a list of offline networking events you could go along to. Get on Google and do a search and see what you find. Make a commitment to go to the events that appeal the most to you.

See also page 137.

Day 27: Set up calls

Reach out to people by making some calls – we rarely use the phone anymore, but it makes it much more personal! Pick up the phone to your business friends, mentors, customers, suppliers – anyone who you'd love to deepen your relationship with.

Relationships are such an important part of business and making a call is a great way to strengthen them.

See also page 108.

Day 28: Review and celebrate

Today is the last day of the challenge! I hope you've discovered and grown a lot over the past 28 days. To finish up the challenge I want you to write down everything you've achieved and learned over the past 28 days. Write down your 'aha' moments, write down your wins, write down what made you happy.

Celebrate these things! Take a moment right now to give yourself a pat on the back for sticking to the challenge and making the commitment to achieve wonderful things.

Write down three things you're most grateful for and feel the gratitude bubble up inside of you.

Then set your intentions for the next 28 days; how are you going to carry on along your entrepreneurial journey?

'A strong woman looks a challenge dead in the eye & gives it a wink.'

Gina Carey

ACKNOWLEDGMENTS

I'd firstly like to thank my dad – thank you for opening my mind and making me believe that anything is possible. You are my entrepreneurial hero and inspiration, and I wouldn't be where I am today if it wasn't for all of our chats and your encouragement. Words can't even express how grateful I am. Mum, thank you for keeping me sane and helping me to stay on top of everything throughout my entire journey. I would be a mess without you. I am so lucky, because you're the most wonderful parents in the world.

To my amazing siblings, Sam, James, and Nick – thank you for all of your help and support along the way. Sam, thank you for all of our chats over a bottle of Oyster Bay, you're always there to listen to my ramblings and make me feel better about everything.

James, thank you for keeping me entertained every day with your jokes and for being the best FEA manager ever! I wouldn't be able to cope without your help and support.

Kelin, my amazing husband, thank you for being my Coach Kelin. You are seriously incredible at inspiring and encouraging me. I'm so lucky that I found such an amazing person to share my life with. You are the best.

My wonderful friends, thank you all so much for your support, encouragement, and friendship over the many years. It means the world to me.

Team FEA, Jess Thenhaus, Michelle Rohr, James Green, Samantha Costello, Andrei Buga – thank you for helping me to build FEA, I'm so glad I found you all, you're amazing and I am forever grateful to you.

FEA members, without you FEA wouldn't exist! You all inspire me every day, thank you for being part of what I've created and thank you for all of your support.

To my commissioning editor, Amy Kiberd, thank you for emailing me and asking if I wanted to write a book with Hay House :-) You made my dream come true! A massive thanks to all of the incredible Hay House UK team – Michelle Pilley, Julie Oughton, Leanne Siu Anastasi, Diane Hill, Tom Cole, Jo Burgess, and Sian Orrell. Also, a huge thanks to Hay House US for supporting me so much with the book – Reid Tracy, Richelle Fredson, Stacy Horowitz, and Lindsay McGinty. Thank you to all of you for your support and help throughout my book journey. I'm so grateful that I got to be part of the Hay House family.

Sandy Draper, thank you for whipping my book into shape with the edit and for putting up with all of my changes! I'm so grateful.

I'd also like to say a big thank you to all of the incredible women I feature in this book. My sister – Samantha Costello – Ailish Lucas (what would I do without you?!) Michelle Rohr (thank you for being my biggest fan, you inspire me so much!), Nikki Elledge Brown (my business bestie, thank you for our chats!), and Kimra Luna (thank you for your boldness, you always inspire me to show up bigger). You're all amazing. Thank you for letting me share your inspiring stories!

I'm so thankful to every single person who has helped me along my journey. Even if I haven't been able to name you all, know that your support means everything to me.

Finally, thank you to you, my wonderful reader. Thank you for coming on this journey with me. I hope it continues for a long time to come!

With so much love and gratitude,

Carrie xx

ABOUT THE AUTHOR
Carrie Green

Carrie Green is the founder of the Female Entrepreneur Association, an online platform dedicated to inspiring and empowering women to turn their ideas into reality and build wildly successful businesses. With over 350,000 women involved worldwide, it's one of the largest support platforms for female entrepreneurs.

Carrie was named an entrepreneurial rising star by HRH The Duke of York after winning The Change Makers Award, and in 2014 she won Entrepreneurs' Champion of the Year Award at the Great British Entrepreneur Awards.

She's been featured on BBC News, and in magazines including *Glamour*, *Grazia*, and *Stylist*. Her TEDx Talk, Programming Your Mind For Success, has had over 2 million views. Carrie is utterly passionate about inspiring women to thrive in business. When she's not focused on this, you will find her spending time with her family and friends, enjoying a glass of white wine, playing the piano, or walking her dogs.

f FemaleEntrepreneurAssociation

You Tube FemaleEntrepreneur

⊙ @iamcarriegreen

👻 @carriegreen_fea

🐦 @iamcarriegreen

🌐 femaleentrepreneurassociation.com

HAY HOUSE

Look within

Join the conversation about latest products,
events, exclusive offers and more.

f Hay House UK

🐦 @HayHouseUK

📷 @hayhouseuk

♥ healyourlife.com

We'd love to hear from you!